IN

DANTE ALIGHIERI was born i
from the lower ranks of the nob                    ed at the
university of Bologna. When he            wenty, he married
Gemma Donati, by whom he had four children. He first met Bice
Portinari, whom he called Beatrice, in 1274, and when she died in
1290 he sought consolation by writing the *Vita nuova* and by
studying philosophy and theology. During this time he also became
involved in the conflict between the Guelf and Ghibelline factions
in Florence; he became a prominent White Guelf and, when the
Black Guelfs came to power in 1302, Dante was, during his absence
from the city, condemned to exile. He took refuge initially in
Verona but eventually, having wandered from place to place, he
settled in Ravenna. While there he completed the *Commedia*,
which he began in about 1307. Dante died in Ravenna in 1321.

ROBIN KIRKPATRICK graduated from Merton College, Oxford.
He has taught courses on Dante's *Commedia* in Hong Kong,
Dublin and – for more than thirty years – at the university of
Cambridge, where he is Fellow of Robinson College and Emeritus
Professor of Italian and English Literatures. His books include
*Dante's Paradiso and the Limitations of Modern Criticism*
(1978), *Dante's Inferno: Difficulty and Dead Poetry* (1987) and
*Dante: The Divine Comedy* (2004), while his own published
poetry includes *Prologue and Palinodes* (1997). His translations
of Dante's *Purgatorio* and *Paradiso* are also available in Penguin
Classics.

in Florence in 1265 into a family
...shire. He may have studied at
...was about twenty. In 1274...

# DANTE ALIGHIERI

# Inferno

*Translated and with notes by*
ROBIN KIRKPATRICK

PENGUIN BOOKS

PENGUIN CLASSICS

Published by the Penguin Group
Penguin Books Ltd, 80 Strand, London WC2R ORL, England
Penguin Group (USA) Inc., 375 Hudson Street, New York, New York 10014, USA
Penguin Group (Canada), 90 Eglinton Avenue East, Suite 700, Toronto, Ontario, Canada M4P 2Y3
(a division of Pearson Penguin Canada Inc.)
Penguin Ireland, 25 St Stephen's Green, Dublin 2, Ireland (a division of Penguin Books Ltd)
Penguin Group (Australia), 707 Collins Street, Melbourne, Victoria 3008, Australia
(a division of Pearson Australia Group Pty Ltd)
Penguin Books India Pvt Ltd, 11 Community Centre, Panchsheel Park, New Delhi – 110 017, India
Penguin Group (NZ), 67 Apollo Drive, Rosedale, Auckland 0632, New Zealand
(a division of Pearson New Zealand Ltd)
Penguin Books (South Africa) (Pty) Ltd, Block D, Rosebank Office Park,
181 Jan Smuts Avenue, Parktown North, Gauteng 2193, South Africa

Penguin Books Ltd, Registered Offices: 80 Strand, London WC2R ORL, England

www.penguin.com

This translation first published in Penguin Classics 2006
The translation published in a revised edition in Penguin Classics 2012
This edition published 2013

021

Translation and notes copyright © Robin Kirkpatrick, 2006, 2012
All rights reserved

The moral right of the editor has been asserted

Set in 10.25/12.25pt PostScript Adobe Sabon
Typeset by Jouve (UK), Milton Keynes
Printed in Great Britain by Clays Ltd, Elcograf S.p.A.

ISBN: 978-0-141-39354-4

www.greenpenguin.co.uk

# Contents

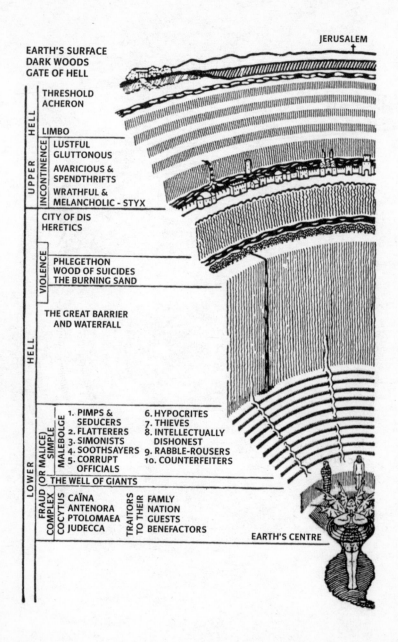

JERUSALEM

EARTH'S SURFACE
DARK WOODS
GATE OF HELL

| | | |
|---|---|---|
| **HELL** (UPPER) | THRESHOLD / ACHERON | |
| | LIMBO | |
| | INCONTINENCE | LUSTFUL |
| | | GLUTTONOUS |
| | | AVARICIOUS & SPENDTHRIFTS |
| | | WRATHFUL & MELANCHOLIC - STYX |

CITY OF DIS
HERETICS

VIOLENCE
PHLEGETHON
WOOD OF SUICIDES
THE BURNING SAND

THE GREAT BARRIER
AND WATERFALL

**HELL (LOWER)**

FRAUD (OR MALICE)

SIMPLE — MALEBOLGE

1. PIMPS & SEDUCERS
2. FLATTERERS
3. SIMONISTS
4. SOOTHSAYERS
5. CORRUPT OFFICIALS
6. HYPOCRITES
7. THIEVES
8. INTELLECTUALLY DISHONEST
9. RABBLE-ROUSERS
10. COUNTERFEITERS

THE WELL OF GIANTS

COMPLEX — COCYTUS

CAÏNA
ANTENORA
PTOLOMAEA
JUDECCA

TRAITORS TO THEIR

FAMILY
NATION
GUESTS
BENEFACTORS

EARTH'S CENTRE

# UPPER HELL

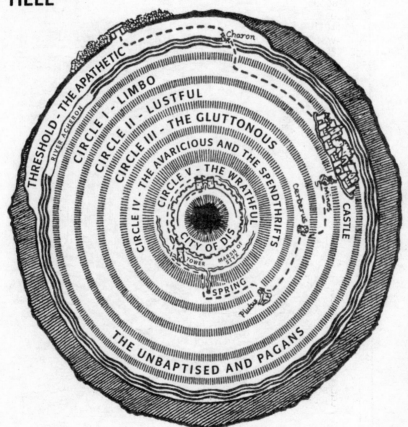

THRESHOLD - THE APATHETIC

RIVER ACHERON

CIRCLE I - LIMBO

CIRCLE II - LUSTFUL

CIRCLE III - THE GLUTTONOUS

CIRCLE IV - THE AVARICIOUS AND THE SPENDTHRIFTS

CIRCLE V - THE WRATHFUL

CITY OF DIS

TOWER

MARSH OF STYX

SPRING

Charon

Cerberus

Dis

CASTLE

Plutus

THE UNBAPTISED AND PAGANS

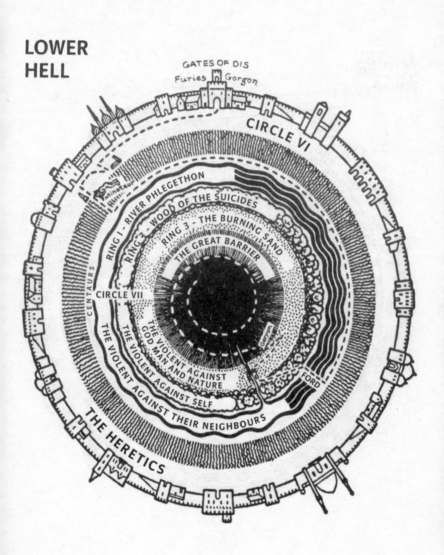

LOWER HELL

GATES OF DIS
Furies    Gorgon

CIRCLE VI

Minotaur

RING 1 - RIVER PHLEGETHON
RING 2 - WOOD OF THE SUICIDES
RING 3 - THE BURNING SAND
THE GREAT BARRIER

CENTAURS

CIRCLE VII

GORGON

THE VIOLENT AGAINST
GOD MAN AND NATURE
THE VIOLENT AGAINST SELF
THE VIOLENT AGAINST THEIR NEIGHBOURS

FORD

THE HERETICS

# LOWER
# HELL

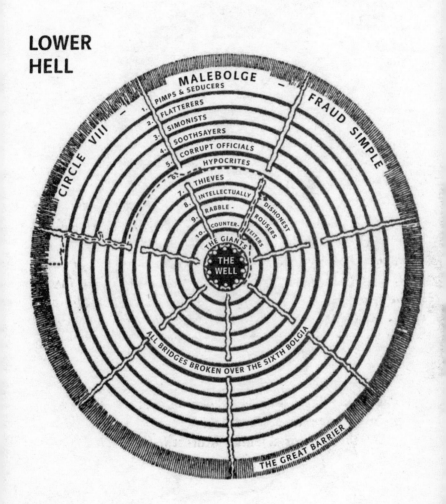

CIRCLE VIII

MALEBOLGE

FRAUD SIMPLE

1. PIMPS & SEDUCERS
2. FLATTERERS
3. SIMONISTS
4. SOOTHSAYERS
5. CORRUPT OFFICIALS
6. HYPOCRITES
7. THIEVES
8. INTELLECTUALLY DISHONEST
9. RABBLE-ROUSERS
10. COUNTER-FEITERS

THE GIANTS

THE WELL

ALL BRIDGES BROKEN OVER THE SIXTH BOLGIA

THE GREAT BARRIER

# LOWER HELL

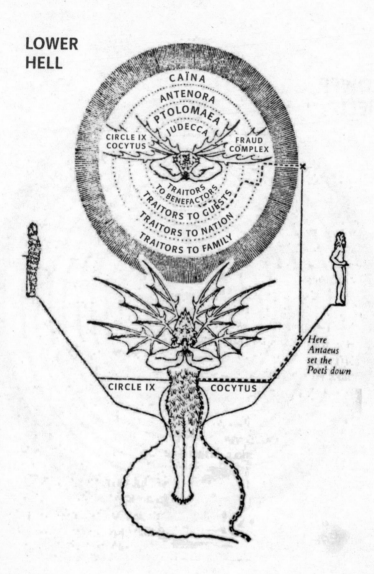

CAÏNA
ANTENORA
PTOLOMAEA
IUDECCA

CIRCLE IX
COCYTUS

FRAUD
COMPLEX

TRAITORS
TO BENEFACTORS
TRAITORS TO GUESTS
TRAITORS TO NATION
TRAITORS TO FAMILY

CIRCLE IX          COCYTUS

*Here
Antaeus
set the
Poets down*

*Inferno*

# CANTO 1

At one point midway on our path in life,   1*
I came around and found myself now searching
through a dark wood, the right way blurred and lost.

How hard it is to say what that wood was,   4
a wilderness, savage, brute, harsh and wild.
Only to think of it renews my fear!

So bitter, that thought, that death is hardly more so.   7
But since my theme will be the good I found there,
I mean to speak of other things I saw.

I do not know, I cannot rightly say,   10
how first I came to be here – so full of sleep,
that moment, abandoning the true way on.

But then, on reaching the foot of a hill   13*
which marked the limit of the dark ravine
that had before so pierced my heart with panic,

I looked to that height and saw its shoulders   16
already clothed in rays from the planet
that leads all others, on any road, aright.

My fears, at this, were somewhat quieted,   19
though terror, awash in the lake of my heart,
had lasted all the night I'd passed in anguish.

And then, like someone labouring for breath   22
who, safely reaching shore from open sea,
still turns and stares across those perilous waves,

so in my mind – my thoughts all fleeing still –   25
I turned around to marvel at that strait
that let no living soul pass through till now.

28*      And then – my weary limbs a little rested –
I started up the lonely scree once more,
the foot that drives me always set the lower.

31*      But look now! Almost as the scarp begins,
a leopard, light and lively, svelte and quick,
its coat displaying a dappled marking.

34      This never ceased to dance before my face.
No. On it came, so bothering my tread
I'd half a mind at every turn to turn.

37      The time, however, was the hour of dawn.
The sun was mounting, and those springtime stars
that rose along with it when Holy Love

40      first moved to being all these lovely things.
So these – the morning hour, the gentle season –
led me to find good reason for my hopes,

43      seeing that creature with its sparkling hide.
Yet not so far that no fear pressed on me,
to see, appearing now, a lion face.

46      This, as it seemed, came on and on towards me
hungrily, its ravening head held high,
so that, in dread, the air around it trembled.

49      And then a wolf. And she who, seemingly,
was gaunt yet gorged on every kind of craving –
and had already blighted many a life –

52      so heavily oppressed my thought with fears,
which spurted even at the sight of her,
I lost all hope of reaching to those heights.

55      We all so willingly record our gains,
until the hour that leads us into loss.
Then every single thought is tears and sadness.

58      So, now, with me. That brute which knows no peace
came ever nearer me and, step by step,
drove me back down to where the sun is mute.

61      As I went, ruined, rushing to that low,
there had, before my eyes, been offered one
who seemed – long silent – to be faint and dry.

Seeing him near in that great wilderness, 64*
to him I screamed my '*Miserere*': 'Save me,
whatever – shadow or truly man – you be.'

His answer came to me: 'No man; a man 67*
I was in times long gone. Of Lombard stock,
my parents both by *patria* were Mantuan.

And I was born, though late, *sub Iulio*. 70
I lived at Rome in good Augustus' day,
in times when all the gods were lying cheats.

I was a poet then. I sang in praise 73
of all the virtues of Anchises' son. From Troy
he came – proud Ilion razed in flame.

But you turn back. Why seek such grief and harm? 76
Why climb no higher up that lovely hill?
The cause and origin of joy shines there.'

'So, could it be,' I answered him (my brow, 79
in shy respect, bent low), 'you are that Virgil,
whose words (a river running full) flow wide?

You are the light and glory of all poets. 82
May this well serve me: my unending care, the love
so great, that's made me search your writings through!

You are my teacher. You, my lord and law. 85
From you alone I took the fine-tuned style
that has, already, brought me so much honour.

See there? That beast! I turned because of that. 88
Help me – your wisdom's known – escape from her.
To every pulsing vein, she brings a tremor.'

Seeing my tears, he answered me: 'There is 91
another road. And that, if you intend
to quit this wilderness, you're bound to take.

That beast – you cry out at the very sight – 94*
lets no one through who passes on her way.
She blocks their progress; and there they all die.

She by her nature is cruel, so vicious 97
she never can sate her voracious will,
but, feasting well, is hungrier than before.

100     She couples, a mate to many a creature,
and will so with more, till at last there comes
the hunting hound that deals her death and pain.

103     He will not feed on dross or cash or gelt,
but thrive in wisdom, virtue and pure love.
Born he shall be between the felt and felt.

106     To all the shores where Italy bows down
(here chaste Camilla died of wounds, Turnus,
Euryalus and Nisus, too), he'll bring true health.

109     Hunting that animal from every town,
at last he'll chase her back once more to Hell,
from which invidia has set her loose.

112     Therefore, considering what's best for you,
I judge that you should follow, I should guide,
and hence through an eternal space lead on.

115     There you shall hear shrill cries of desperation,
and see those spirits, mourning ancient pain,
who all cry out for death to come once more.

118     And then you'll see those souls who live in fire,
content to hope – whenever that time comes –
they too will be among the blessed choirs.

121     To which if you shall ever wish to rise,
a soul will come far worthier than me.
I must, at parting, leave you in her care.

124     Reigning on high, there is an Emperor
who, since I was a rebel to His law,
will not allow His city as my goal.

127     He rules there, sovereign over every part.
There stands His capital, His lofty throne.
Happy the one He chooses for His own.'

130     'Poet,' I answered, 'by that God whose name
you never knew, I beg you, I entreat –
so I may flee this ill and worse – that you

133     now lead me on to where you've spoken of,
to find the gate where now Saint Peter stands,
and all those souls that you say are so sad.'

136     He made to move; and I came close behind.

# CANTO 2

Daylight was leaving us, and darkened air     1*
drawing those creatures that there are on earth
from all their labours. I alone, I was
    the only one preparing, as in war,     4
to onward-march and bear the agony
that thought will now unfailingly relate.
    I call the Muses. You great Heights of Mind     7
bring help to me. You, Memory, wrote down all I saw.
Now shall be seen the greatness of your power.
    'You,' I began, 'my poet and my guide,     10
look at me hard. Am I in spirit strong enough
for you to trust me on this arduous road?
    As you once told, the sire of Silvius     13*
travelled, though still in fragile flesh, to realms
immortal, and his senses all alive.
    Nor will it seem (to those of intellect)     16
unfitting if the enemy of ill
should thus so greatly favour him, recalling
    what flowed from him, his name and who he was.     19
He was ordained, in empyrean skies,
father of Rome – its noble heart and empire.
    To speak the truth: that city – and the sphere     22
it ruled – was founded as the sacred seat
for all inheritors of great Saint Peter.
    You have proclaimed the glory of that march.     25
He on his way heard prophecies that led
to all his triumphs and the papal stole.

8

28\*     And then Saint Paul, the chosen Vessel, came –
to carry back a strengthening of that faith
from which salvation always must begin.

31     But me? Why me? Who says I can? I'm not
your own Aeneas. I am not Saint Paul.
No one – not me! – could think I'm fit for this.

34     Surrendering, I'll say I'll come. I fear
this may be lunacy. You, though, are wise.
You know me better than my own words say.'

37     And so – as though unwanting every want,
so altering all at every altering thought,
now drawing back from everything begun –

40     I stood there on the darkened slope, fretting
away from thought to thought the bold intent
that seemed so very urgent at the outset.

43     'Supposing I have heard your words aright,'
the shadow of that noble mind replied,
'your heart is struck with ignominious dread.

46     This, very often, is the stumbling block
that turns a noble enterprise off-course –
as beasts will balk at shadows falsely seen.

49     I mean that you should free yourself from fear,
and therefore I will say why first I came,
and what – when first I grieved for you – I heard.

52\*     With those I was whose lives are held in poise.
And then I heard a lady call – so blessed,
so beautiful – I begged her tell me all she wished.

55     Her eyes were shining brighter than the stars.
Then gently, softly, calmly, she began,
speaking, as angels might, in her own tongue:

58     "You, Mantuan, so courteous in spirit,
your fame endures undimmed throughout the world,
and shall endure as still that world moves onwards.

61     A man most dear to me – though not to fate –
is so entrammelled on the lonely hill
that now he turns, all terror, from the way.

My fear must be he's so bewildered there                    64
that – hearing all I've heard of him in Heaven –
I rise too late to bring him any aid.

Now make your way. With all your eloquence,                 67
and all that his deliverance demands,
lend him your help so I shall be consoled.

For me you'll go, since I am Beatrice.                      70
And I have come from where I long to be.
Love is my mover, source of all I say.

When I again appear before my Lord,                         73
then I shall often speak your praise to Him."
She now fell silent. I began to speak:

"Lady of worth and truth, through you alone                 76
the human race goes far beyond that bourne
set by the moon's sphere, smallest of all the skies.

To me, so welcome is your least command,                    79
I'd be too slow had I obeyed by now.
You need no more declare to me your will.

But tell me why you take so little care                     82
and, down to this dead middle point, you leave
the spacious circle where you burn to go."

"Since you desire to know so inwardly,                      85
then briefly," she replied, "I'll tell you why
I feel no dread at entering down here.

We dread an object when (but only when)                     88
that object has the power to do some harm.
Nothing can otherwise occasion fear.

I was created by the grace of God –                         91
and so untouched by all your wretchedness.
Nor can the flames of this great fire assail me.

In Heaven, a Lady, gracious, good and kind,                 94*
grieves at the impasse that I send you to,
and, weeping, rives the high, unbending rule.

She called Lucia, seeking her reply.                        97
'Your faithful one,' she said to her, 'has now
great need of you. I give him to your care.'

100 Lucia is the enemy of harm.
Leaving her place, she came at once to where
I sat – Rachel, long-famed, along with me.

103  'You, Beatrice, are, in truth, God's praise.
Why not,' she said, 'make haste to him? He loves you,
and, loving you, he left the common herd.

106  Can you not hear the pity of his tears?
Do you not see the death that beats him down,
swirling in torrents that no sea could boast?'

109  No one on earth has ever run more rapidly
to seek advantage or else flee from harm,
than I in coming – when her words were done –

112  down from that throne of happiness, to trust
in your great words, their dignity and truth.
These honour you and those who hear you speak."

115  When she had said her say, in tears, she turned
her eyes away – which shone as she was weeping.
And this made me far quicker still for you.

118  So now, as she had willed, I made my way,
to raise you from the face of that brute beast
that stole your pathway up that lovely hill.

121  What is it, then? What's wrong? Why still delay?
Why fondle in your heart such feebleness?
Why wait? Be forthright, brave and resolute.

124  Three ladies of the court of Paradise,
in utmost happiness watch over you.
My own words promise you the utmost good.'

127  As little flowers bend low on freezing nights,
closed tight, but then, as sunlight whitens them,
grow upright on their stems and fully open,

130  now so did I. My wearied powers reviving,
there ran such wealth of boldness to my heart
that openly – all new and free – I now began:

133  'How quick in compassion her aid to me!
And you – so courteous, prompt to accede
to all the words of truth that she has offered!

You, as you speak, have so disposed my heart 136
in keen desire to journey on the way
that I return to find my first good purpose.
    Set off! A single will inspires us both. 139
You are my lord, my leader and true guide.'
All this I said to him as he moved on.
    I entered on that deep and wooded road. 142

# CANTO 3

1*      'Through me you go to the grief-wracked city.
Through me to everlasting pain you go.
Through me you go and pass among lost souls.

4       Justice inspired my exalted Creator.
I am a creature of the Holiest Power,
of Wisdom in the Highest and of Primal Love.

7       Nothing till I was made was made, only
eternal beings. And I endure eternally.
Surrender as you enter every hope you have.'

10      These were the words that – written in dark tones –
I saw there, on the summit of a door.
I turned: 'Their meaning, sir, for me is hard.'

13      And he in answering (as though he understood):
'You needs must here surrender all your doubts.
All taint of cowardice must here be dead.

16*     We now have come where, as I have said, you'll see
in suffering the souls of those who've lost
the good that intellect desires to win.'

19      And then he placed his hand around my own,
he smiled, to give me some encouragement,
and set me on to enter secret things.

22      Sighing, sobbing, moans and plaintive wailing
all echoed here through air where no star shone,
and I, as this began, began to weep.

25      Discordant tongues, harsh accents of horror,
tormented words, the twang of rage, strident
voices, the sound, as well, of smacking hands,

together these all stirred a storm that swirled                    28
for ever in the darkened air where no time was,
as sand swept up in breathing spires of wind.

I turned, my head tight-bound in confusion,                        31
to say to my master: 'What is it that I hear?
Who can these be, so overwhelmed by pain?'

'This baleful condition is one,' he said,                          34*
'that grips those souls whose lives, contemptibly,
were void alike of honour and ill fame.

These all co-mingle with a noisome choir                           37
of angels who – not rebels, yet not true
to God – existed for themselves alone.

To keep their beauty whole, the Heavens spurned them.              40
Nor would the depths of Hell receive them in,
lest truly wicked souls boast over them.'

And I: 'What can it be, so harsh, so heavy,                        43
that draws such loud lamentings from these crowds?'
And he replied: 'My answer can be brief:

These have no hope that death will ever come.                      46
And so degraded is the life they lead
all look with envy on all other fates.

The world allows no glory to their name.                           49
Mercy and Justice alike despise them.
Let us not speak of them. Look, then pass on.'

I did look, intently. I saw a banner                               52
running so rapidly, whirling forwards,
that nothing, it seemed, would ever grant a pause.

Drawn by that banner was so long a trail                           55*
of men and women I should not have thought
that death could ever have unmade so many.

A few I recognized. And then I saw –                               58*
and knew beyond all doubt – the shadow of the one
who made, from cowardice, the great denial.

So I, at that instant, was wholly sure                             61
this congregation was that worthless mob
loathsome alike to God and their own enemies.

64 These wretched souls were never truly live.
They now went naked and were sharply spurred
by wasps and hornets, thriving all around.

67 The insects streaked the face of each with blood.
Mixing with tears, the lines ran down; and then
were garnered at their feet by filthy worms.

70 And when I'd got myself to look beyond,
others, I saw, were ranged along the bank
of some great stream. 'Allow me, sir,' I said,

73 'to know who these might be. What drives them on,
and makes them all (as far, in this weak light,
as I discern) so eager for the crossing?'

76 'That will, of course, be clear to you,' he said,
'when once our footsteps are set firm upon
the melancholic shores of Acheron.'

79 At this – ashamed, my eyes cast humbly down,
fearing my words had weighed on him too hard –
I held my tongue until we reached the stream.

82* Look now! Towards us in a boat there came
an old man, yelling, hair all white and aged,
'Degenerates! Your fate is sealed! Cry woe!

85 Don't hope you'll ever see the skies again!
I'm here to lead you to the farther shore,
into eternal shadow, heat and chill.

88 And you there! You! Yes, you, the living soul!
Get right away from this gang! These are dead.'
But then, on seeing that I did not move:

91 'You will arrive by other paths and ports.
You'll start your journey from a different beach.
A lighter hull must carry you across.'

94 'Charon,' my leader, 'don't torment yourself.
For this is willed where all is possible
that is willed there. And so demand no more.'

97 The fleecy wattles of the ferry man –
who plied across the liverish swamp, eyeballs
encircled by two wheels of flame – fell mute.

But not the other souls. Naked and drained,       100
their complexions changed. Their teeth began
(hearing his raw command) to gnash and grind.

They raged, blaspheming God and their own kin,    103
the human race, the place and time, the seed
from which they'd sprung, the day that they'd been born.

And then they came together all as one,      106
wailing aloud along the evil margin
that waits for all who have no fear of God.

Charon the demon, with his hot-coal eyes,     109
glared what he meant to do. He swept all in.
He struck at any dawdler with his oar.

In autumn, leaves are lifted, one by one,     112*
away until the branch looks down and sees
its tatters all arrayed upon the ground.

In that same way did Adam's evil seed      115
hurtle, in sequence, from the river rim,
as birds that answer to their handler's call.

Then off they went, to cross the darkened flood.   118
And, long before they'd landed over there,
another flock assembled in their stead.

Attentively, my master said: 'All those,      121
dear son, who perish in the wrath of God,
meet on this shore, wherever they were born.

And they are eager to be shipped across.     124
Justice of God so spurs them all ahead
that fear in them becomes that sharp desire.

But no good soul will ever leave from here.    127
And so when Charon thus complains of you,
you may well grasp the sense that sounds within.'

His words now done, the desolate terrain     130
trembled with such great violence that the thought
soaks me once more in a terrified sweat.

The tear-drenched earth gave out a gust of wind,   133
erupting in a flash of bright vermilion,
that overwhelmed all conscious sentiment.

I fell like someone gripped by sudden sleep.    136

# CANTO 4

1      Thunder rolling heavily in my head
shattered my deep sleep. Startled, I awoke –
as though just shaken in some violent grip.

4      And then once more my sight grew firm and fixed.
Now upright and again afoot, I scanned,
intently, all around to view where I might be.

7      I found I'd reached – and this is true – the edge
of the abyss, that cavern of grief and pain
that rings a peal of endless miseries.

10     The pit, so dark, so wreathed in cloud, went down
so far that – peering towards its deepest floor –
I still could not discern a single thing.

13     'Let us descend,' the poet now began,
'and enter this blind world.' His face was pale.
'I shall go first. Then you come close behind.'

16     I was aware of his altered colour.
'How can I come, when you,' I said, 'my strength
in every time of doubt, are terrified?'

19     'It is the agony,' he answered me,
'of those below that paints my features thus –
not fear, as you suppose it is, but pity.

22     Let us go on. The long road spurs our pace.'
So now he set himself – and me as well –
to enter Circle One, which skirts the emptiness.

25     Here in the dark (where only hearing told)
there were no tears, no weeping, only sighs
that caused a trembling in the eternal air –

sighs drawn from sorrowing, although no pain.                    28
This weighs on all of them, those multitudes
of speechless children, women and full-grown men.

'You do not ask,' my teacher in his goodness said,              31
'who all these spirits are that you see here?
Do not, I mean, go further till you know:

these never sinned. And some attained to merit.                 34
But merit falls far short. None was baptized.
None passed the gate, in your belief, to faith.

They lived before the Christian age began.                       37
They paid no reverence, as was due to God.
And in this number I myself am one.

For such deficiencies, no other crime,                           40
we all are lost yet only suffer harm
through living in desire, but hopelessly.'

At hearing this, great sorrow gripped my heart.                  43
For many persons of the greatest worth
were held, I knew, suspended on this strip.

'Tell me, sir, tell me, my dearest teacher,'                     46*
so I began, determined – on a point
of faith, which routs all error – to be sure,

'has anyone, by merit of his own                                 49
or else another's, left here then been blessed?'
And he, who read the sense my words had hid,

answered: 'I still was new to this strange state                 52
when, now advancing, I beheld a power
whose head was crowned with signs of victory.

He led away the shadow of our primal sire,                       55
shades of his offspring, Abel and Noah,
Moses, who uttered (and observed) the law,

of Abraham the patriarch, David the king,                        58
Israel, his father and his own twelve sons,
with Rachel, too, for whom he laboured long,

and many more besides. All these He blessed.                     61
This too I mean you'll know: until these were,
no human soul had ever been redeemed.'

64      Speak as he might, our journey did not pause,
but on we went, and onward, through the wood –
the wood, I mean, of spirits thronging round.

67      Our steps were still not far from where, in sleep,
I fell, when now, ahead, I saw a fire
that overcame a hemisphere of shade.

70      From this we were, as yet, some paces off,
but not so far that I should fail to see
that men of honour made this place their own.

73      'Honour you bring, my lord, to art and learning.
Inform me who these are – their honour great –
who stand apart in some way from the rest.'

76      He answered me: 'The honour of their name
rings clear for those, like you, who live above,
and here gains favour out of Heaven's grace.'

79      And then there came upon my ear a voice:
'Honour be his, the poet in the heights.
His shadow now returns which had departed.'

82      The voice was still and silent once again.
And now, I saw, there came four noble shades,
no sorrow in their countenance, nor joy.

85      My teacher – that good man – began to speak:
'Look on. Behold the one who, sword in hand,
precedes, as their true lord, the other three.

88*     This is that sovereign Homer, poet.
Horace the satirist is next to come,
Ovid is third. Then (see!) there is Lucan.

91      All these, by right, must duly share with me
the name that sounded in that single voice.
They do me honour thus, and thus do well.'

94      And so I saw, assembling there as one,
the lovely college of that lord of song
whose verses soar like eagles over all.

97      Some little time they talked among themselves,
then turned to me and offered signs of greeting.
On seeing all of this, my teacher smiled.

And greater honour still they paid me now:  100
they summoned me to join them in their ranks.
I came and walked as sixth among such wisdom.

So on we went to reach the dome of light  103
and spoke of things which, proper where I was,
are relegated, rightly, here to silence.

We reached the footings of a noble fort,  106
circled around by seven curtain walls
and also, as its moat, a lovely stream.

We passed this brook as though it were dry land.  109
Through seven gates I went with these five sages.
We then came out upon a verdant lawn.

Here there were some whose eyes were firm and grave –  112
all, in demeanour, of authority –
who seldom spoke; their tones were calm and gentle.

And so we drew aside and found a space,  115
illuminated, open, high and airy,
where all of these were able to be seen.

And there, across that bright enamelled green,  118
these ancient heroes were displayed to me.
And I within myself am still raised high

at what I saw: Electra, many round her.  121*
Hector I recognized, Aeneas, too,
and Caesar in arms, with his hawk-like eyes.

Camilla I saw and Penthesilea,  124
and King Latinus on the other side –
his daughter seated with him, his Lavinia.

Brutus (he drove proud Tarquin out), Lucrece  127
and Julia, Marcia, Cornelia – all these I saw,
and there alone, apart, the sultan Saladin.

And then – my brow raised higher still – I saw,  130*
among his family of philosophers,
the master of all those who think and know.

To him all look in wonder, all in honour.  133
And, closer to his side than all the rest,
I now saw Socrates, I saw now Plato,

136     and one, Democritus, who claims the world is chance,
Diogenes and Tales, Anaxagoras,
Empedocles, Heraclitus and Zeno.

139     Then one I saw who gathered healing herbs –
I mean good Dioscorides. Orpheus I saw,
and Seneca the moralist, Linus, Tully,

142     Euclid (geometer) and Ptolemy,
Hippocrates, Avicenna and Galen,
Averroes, too, who made the *Commentary*.

145     I cannot here draw portraits of them all;
my lengthy subject presses me ahead,
and saying often falls far short of fact.

148     That company of six declines to two.
My lord in wisdom leads a different way,
out of that quiet into trembling air.

151     And nothing, where I now arrive, is shining.

# CANTO 5

And so from Circle One I now went down                    1
deeper, to Circle Two, which bounds a lesser space
and therefore greater suffering. Its sting is misery.

Minos stands there – horribly there – and barking.        4*
He, on the threshold, checks degrees of guilt,
then judges and dispatches with his twirling tail.

I mean that every ill-begotten creature,                  7
when summoned here, confesses everything.
And he (his sense of sin is very fine)

perceives what place in Hell best suits each one,         10
and coils his tail around himself to tell
the numbered ring to which he'll send them down.

Before him, always, stands a crowd of souls.              13
By turns they go, each one, for sentencing.
Each pleads, attends – and then is tipped below.

'You there, arriving at this house of woe,'               16
so, when he saw me there, the judge spoke forth,
(to interrupt a while his formal role),

'watch as you enter – and in whom you trust.              19
Don't let yourself be fooled by this wide threshold.'
My leader's thrust: 'This yelling! Why persist?

Do not impede him on his destined way.                    22
For this is willed where all is possible
that is willed there. And so demand no more.'

But now the tones of pain, continuing,                    25
demand I hear them out. And now I've come
where grief and weeping pierce me at the heart.

28 And so I came where light is mute, a place
that moans as oceans do impelled by storms,
surging, embattled in conflicting squalls.

31 The swirling wind of Hell will never rest.
It drags these spirits onwards in its force.
It chafes them – rolling, clashing – grievously.

34 Then, once they reach the point from which they fell . . .
screams, keening cries, the agony of all,
and all blaspheming at the Holy Power.

37 Caught in this torment, as I understood,
were those who – here condemned for carnal sin –
made reason bow to their instinctual bent.

40 As starlings on the wing in winter chills
are borne along in wide and teeming flocks,
so on these breathing gusts the evil souls.

43 This way and that and up and down they're borne.
Here is no hope of any comfort ever,
neither of respite nor of lesser pain.

46 And now, as cranes go singing lamentations
and form themselves through air in long-drawn lines,
coming towards me, trailing all their sorrows,

49 I saw new shadows lifted by this force.
'Who are these people? Tell me, sir,' I said,
'why black air scourges them so viciously.'

52* 'The first of those whose tale you wish to hear,'
he answered me without a moment's pause,
'governed as empress over diverse tongues.

55 She was so wracked by lust and luxury,
licentiousness was legal under laws she made –
to lift the blame that she herself incurred.

58 This is Semiramis. Of her one reads
that she, though heir to Ninus, was his bride.
Her lands were those where now the Sultan reigns.

61 The other, lovelorn, slew herself and broke
her vow of faith to Sichaeus's ashes.
And next, so lascivious, Cleopatra.

Helen. You see? Because of her, a wretched     64
waste of years went by. See! Great Achilles.
He fought with love until his final day.

Paris you see, and Tristan there.' And more     67
than a thousand shadows he numbered, naming
them all, whom Love had led to leave our life.

Hearing that man of learning herald thus     70
these chevaliers of old, and noble ladies,
pity oppressed me and I was all but lost.

'How willingly,' I turned towards the poet,     73*
'I'd speak to those two there who go conjoined
and look to be so light upon the wind.'

And he to me: 'You'll see them clearer soon.     76
When they are closer, call to them. Invoke
the love that draws them on, and they will come.'

The wind had swept them nearer to us now.     79
I moved to them in words: 'Soul-wearied creatures!
Come, if none forbids, to us and, breathless, speak.'

As doves, when called by their desires, will come –     82
wings spreading high – to settle on their nest,
borne through the air by their own steady will,

so these two left the flock where Dido is.     85
They came, approaching through malignant air,
so strong for them had been my feeling cry.

'Our fellow being, gracious, kind and good!     88*
You, on your journeying through this bruised air,
here visit two who tinged the world with blood.

Suppose the Sovereign of the Universe     91
were still our friend, we'd pray He grant you peace.
You pity so the ill perverting us.

Whatever you may please to hear or say,     94
we, as we hear, we, as we speak, assent,
so long – as now they do – these winds stay silent.

My native place is set along those shores     97
through which the river Po comes down, to be
at last at peace with all its tributaries.

100     Love, who so fast brings flame to generous hearts,
        seized him with feeling for the lovely form,
        now torn from me. The harm of how still rankles.

103     Love, who no loved one pardons love's requite,
        seized me for him so strongly in delight
        that, as you see, he does not leave me yet.

106*    Love drew us onwards to consuming death.
        Cain's ice awaits the one who quenched our lives.'
        These words, borne on to us from them, were theirs.

109     And when I heard these spirits in distress,
        I bowed my eyes and held them low, until,
        at length, the poet said: 'What thoughts are these?'

112     I, answering in the end, began: 'Alas,
        how many yearning thoughts, what great desire,
        have led them through such sorrow to their fate?'

115     And turning to them now I came to say:
        'Francesca, how your suffering saddens me!
        Sheer pity brings me to the point of tears.

118     But tell me this: the how of it – and why –
        that Love, in sweetness of such sighing hours,
        permitted you to know these doubtful pangs.'

121*    To me she said: 'There is no sorrow greater
        than, in times of misery, to hold at heart
        the memory of happiness. (Your teacher knows.)

124     And yet, if you so deeply yearn to trace
        the root from which the love we share first sprang,
        then I shall say – and speak as though in tears.

127     One day we read together, for pure joy
        how Lancelot was taken in Love's palm.
        We were alone. We knew no suspicion.

130     Time after time, the words we read would lift
        our eyes and drain all colour from our faces.
        A single point, however, vanquished us.

133     For when at last we read the longed-for smile
        of Guinevere – at last her lover kissed –
        he, who from me will never now depart,

    touched his kiss, trembling to my open mouth.      136
This book was *Galehault* – pander-penned, the pimp!
That day we read no further down those lines.'

    And all the while, as one of them spoke on,      139
the other wept, and I, in such great pity,
fainted away as though I were to die.

    And now I fell as bodies fall, for dead.      142

# CANTO 6

1  As now I came once more to conscious mind –
closed in those feelings for the kindred souls
that had, in sudden sadness, overcome me –

4  wherever I might turn I saw – wherever
I might move, look around or settle my gaze –
new forms of torment, new tormented souls.

7  I am in Circle Three. And rain falls there,
endlessly, chill, accursed and heavy,
its rate and composition never new.

10  Snow, massive hailstones, black, tainted water
pour down in sheets through tenebrae of air.
The earth absorbs it all and stinks, revoltingly.

13*  Cerberus, weird and monstrously cruel,
barks from his triple throats in cur-like yowls
over the heads of those who lie there, drowned.

16  His eyes vermilion, beard a greasy black,
his belly broad, his fingers all sharp-nailed,
he mauls and skins, then hacks in four, these souls.

19  From all of them, rain wrings a wet-dog howl.
They squirm, as flank screens flank. They twist, they turn,
and then – these vile profanities – they turn again.

22  That reptile Cerberus now glimpsed us there.
He stretched his jaws; he showed us all his fangs.
And me? No member in my frame stayed still!

25  My leader, bending with his palms wide-spanned,
scooped dirt in each, and then – his fists both full –
hurled these as sops down all three ravening throats.

A hungry mongrel – yapping, thrusting out,    28
intent on nothing but the meal to come –
is silent only when its teeth sink in.

In that same way, with three repulsive muzzles,    31
the demon Cerberus. His thunderous growlings
stunned these souls. They wished themselves stone deaf.

Over such shadows, flat in that hard rain,    34
we travelled onwards still. Our tread now fell
on voided nothings only seeming men.

Across the whole terrain these shades were spread,    37
except that one, at seeing us pass by,
sat, on the sudden, upright and then cried:

'You there! Drawn onwards through this stretch of Hell,    40*
tell me you know me. Say so, if so you can.
You! Made as man before myself unmade.'

And I replied: 'The awful pain you feel    43
perhaps has cancelled you from memory.
Till now, it seems, I've never even seen you.

Then tell me who you are, and why you dwell    46
in such a place? And why a pain like this?
Others may well be worse, none so disgusting.'

And he: 'That burgh of yours – that sack of bile    49
that brims by now to overflow – I lived
as hers throughout my own fine-weather years.

You knew me, like your city friends, as Hoggo.    52
So here I am, condemned for gullet sins,
lying, you see, squashed flat by battering rain.

I'm not alone in misery of soul.    55
These all lie subject to the self-same pain.
Their guilt is mine.' He spoke no further word.

'Hoggo, your heavy labours,' I replied,    58
'weigh on me hard and prompt my heavy tears.
But tell me, if you can, where they'll all end,

the citizens of that divided town?    61
Is there among them any honest man?
Why is that place assailed by so much strife?'

64     His answer was: 'From each side, long harangues.
And then to blood. The Wildwood boys
will drive the others out. They'll do great harm.

67     But then, within the span of three brief suns,
that side will fall and others rise and thrive,
spurred on by one who now just coasts between.

70     For quite some time they'll hold their heads up high
and grind the others under heavy weights,
however much, for shame, these weep and writhe.

73     Of this lot, two are honest yet not heard.
For pride and avarice and envy are
the three fierce sparks that set all hearts ablaze.'

76     With this, his tear-drenched song now reached an end.
But I to him: 'I still want more instruction.
This gift I ask of you: please do say more.

79*    Tegghiaio, Farinata – men of rank –
Mosca, Arrigo, Rusticucci, too,
and others with their minds on noble deeds,

82     tell me, so I may know them, where they are.
For I am gripped by great desire, to tell
if Heaven holds them sweet – or poisonous Hell.'

85     And he: 'These dwell among the blackest souls,
loaded down deep by sins of differing types.
If you sink far enough, you'll see them all.

88     But when you walk once more where life is sweet,
bring me, I beg, to others in remembrance.
No more I'll say, nor answer any more.'

91     His forward gaze now twisted to a squint.
He stared at me a little, bent his head,
then fell face down and joined his fellow blind.

94     My leader now addressed me: 'He'll not stir
until the trumpets of the angels sound,
at which his enemy, True Power, will come.

97     Then each will see once more his own sad tomb,
and each, once more, assume its flesh and figure,
each hear the rumbling thunder roll for ever.'

So on we fared across that filthy blend          100
of rain and shadow spirit, slow in step,
touching a little on the life to come.

    Concerning which, 'These torments, sir,' I said,    103
'when judgement has been finally proclaimed –
will these increase or simmer just the same?'

    'Return,' he said, 'to your first principles:    106*
when anything (these state) becomes more perfect,
then all the more it feels both good and pain.

    Albeit these accursed men will not    109
achieve perfection full and true, they still,
beyond that Day, will come to sharper life.'

    So, circling on the curve around that path,    112
we talked of more than I shall here relate,
but reached the brow, from which the route descends,

    and found there Plutus, the tremendous foe.    115*

# CANTO 7

<sup></sup>

1*     *'Popoi Satan, popoi Satan! Alezorul!'*
So Plutus – shrill voice clucking on – began.
But Virgil, wise and noble, knowing all,

4       spoke out, to comfort me: 'Let not your fears
occasion you distress. Despite his powers,
he cannot steal your right to scale this rock face.'

7       And then he turned to meet those rabid lips.
'Silence, you execrable wolf!' he said.
'May fury gnaw you inwardly away.

10*     To these dark depths, with every right he treads.
All this is willed where Michael, in the heights,
avenged the rapine wrought by prideful hordes.'

13      As sails, inflated by a furious wind,
fall in a tangle when the main mast snaps,
so too he flopped, this predator, to ground.

16      Then downwards to the seventh sink we went,
advancing further down the curving wall
that bags up all the evil of the universe.

19      God in all justice! I saw there so many
new forms of travail, so tightly crammed. By whom?
How can our guilt so rend and ruin us?

22*     Over Charybdis, the sea surge swirls
and shatters on the swell it clashes with.
So must these people dance their morisco.

25      I saw, in numbers greater than elsewhere,
two factions, hollering, this one to that,
who rolled great boulders, thrust by rib and tit.

Their stones would clash. Then wheeling they'd retreat    28
and yell, across their shoulders, cry and counter-cry.
'You miser! Why?' 'Why fling it all away?'

So back along that dismal curve they went,    31
to reach, at either end, the diametric points,
still screaming shamefully insulting chants.

Arriving – each round his half-circle – back,    34
each whisked around to tilt against the next other.
At this – my heart transfixed, or very nearly:

'Sir,' I spoke up, 'make clear to me what folk    37
these are, and whether – to our left – all those
with tonsured scalps could really have been clerics.'

'Without exception, all of these,' he said,    40
'when first they lived, had such strabismic minds
they'd bear no check or measure on expense.

And when they reach the two points in the round    43*
where converse crimes uncouple each from each,
they bark their meaning out and sound it clear.

Clerics they were – all those whose heads aren't dressed    46
with shaggy hair. All popes – or cardinals.
In that lot, avarice displays its worst.'

'Well, sir,' I said, 'in any group like this,    49
I surely ought to recognize some few
who bore in life the taint of this disease.'

'You seek,' he said, 'to form an idle thought.    52
The mindless lives that made them all so foul
darken them now against all acts of mind.

Both, to eternity, will buck and butt.    55
These from their tombs will rise with fists tight shut,
the others with their curly manes cropped short.

Their frenzied sprees or febrile hoardings-up    58
have wrung from them the beauty of the world,
and brought them firmly to this ugly brawl.

You now can see, dear son, the short-lived pranks    61
that goods consigned to Fortune's hand will play,
causing such squabbles in the human ranks.

64      For all the gold that lies beneath the moon –
        or all that ever did lie there – would bring
        no respite to these worn-out souls, not one.'

67      'Please tell me, sir,' I said, a little more,
        'what can it be, this Fortune that you touch on,
        that clasps all earthly goods between its claws?'

70      And he to me: 'You idiotic creatures,
        so greatly hurt by your own ignorance!
        Feed on my words. I'd have you grasp their sense.

73*     He who transcends in wisdom all that is,
        wrought every sphere and gave to each a guide,
        so every part shines out to every part

76      always in equal distribution of light.
        So, too, above the splendours of the world,
        He set a sovereign minister, ordained to move –

79      in permutations at the proper time –
        vain goods from tribe to tribe, from blood to blood,
        in ways from which no human wisdom hides.

82      And this is why, where one race rules supreme,
        another faints and languishes: they all pursue
        her judgements, secret as a snake in grass.

85      Your powers of mind cannot contend with her.
        She, looking forwards, will pronounce her law,
        advancing, as do other gods, her own domain.

88      Her permutations never come to rest.
        It is necessity that makes her quick,
        so thick they come by turns to meet their fate.

91      She is the one so often crossed and cursed
        by those who, rightly, ought to sing her praise,
        yet vilify her name and speak her ill.

94      But she, a holy being, pays no heed.
        Happy, with all the other primal powers,
        she turns her sphere, rejoicing in beatitude.

97*     So let us now go down to greater pain.
        The stars that rose when I first stirred now fall.
        We cannot stay too long. That is forbidden.'

Cutting across the circle, we approached                          100
the margins of a spring – which, seething, spilled
and ran from there along an outer sluice.

The waters here were darker, far, than perse.               103
So, on – accompanied by murky waves –
downwards we travelled by a weirder route.

Into a swamp (by name, the loathsome Styx)             106
this melancholy brook makes way, and finds
the foot of those malignant, grey-black slopes.

As there I stood, intent and wondering,                        109
I saw there, plunged within that stagnant fen,
a peevish people, naked, caked with mud.

Each battered each – and not with fists alone,            112
also with head butts, kicks and charging chests.
Their teeth, too, tore them, bit by bit, to shreds.

'You witness now,' my gentle teacher said,                 115*
'the souls of those whom anger overthrew.
And this I'd also have you know: be sure,

beneath the surface of this slick are some              118
whose sighs – as you can see at every turn –
now aerate that pullulating film.

So, stuck there fast in slime, they hum: "Mournful      121
we were. Sunlight rejoices the balmy air.
We, though, within ourselves nursed sullen fumes,

and come to misery in this black ooze."                  124
That is the hymn each gurgles in his gorge,
unable to articulate a single phrase.'

So, on around this sour, revolting pit,                     127
between the sludge and arid rock, we swung
our arc, eyes bent on those who gulped that slop.

We reached, in fine, the bottom of a tower.            130

# CANTO 8

1  And so I say (continuing) that, long before
we reached the bottom of that lofty tower,
our eyes had travelled upwards to its summit,

4  drawn by a pair of tiny flames, set there –
as now we saw – to signal to a third,
so far away the eye could hardly grasp it.

7  I turned towards the ocean of all wisdom:
'What do they mean?' I said to him. 'What answer
does the farther fire now give? Who makes these signs?'

10  And he: 'Across these waves of foaming mire,
you may already glimpse what they've been waiting for,
unless it still goes hidden by these marshy fumes.'

13  No bow string ever shot through air an arrow
rapider than now, at speed, I saw come on
towards us there, a mean little vessel,

16  within it – as pilot plying these waters –
a single galley man who strained the oar,
squealing: 'You fiend! You've got it coming now!'

19*  'Phlegyas, Phlegyas!' my master said.
'Your screams and shouts have, this time, little point.
We're yours – but only while we cross this marsh.'

22  Like someone hearing that a massive hoax
has just, to his disgruntlement, been pulled on him,
so Phlegyas now stood, in pent-up rage.

25  My lord stepped down, and, entering the boat,
he made me, in my turn, embark behind.
The hull seemed laden only when I did.

At once – my leader boarded, me as well –                    28
the ancient prow put out. It sawed the waves
more deeply than it would with other crews.

So, rushing forwards on that lifeless slick,                 31*
there jerked up, fronting me, one brimming slime
who spoke: 'So who – you come too soon! – are you?'

And my riposte: 'I come, perhaps; I'll not remain.           34
But who might you be, brutishly befouled?'
His answer was: 'Just look at me. I'm one

who weeps.' And I to him: 'Weep on. In grief,                37
may you remain, you spirit of damnation!
I know who *you* are, filth as you may be.'

And then he stretched both hands towards our gunwales.       40
My teacher, though – alert – soon drove him back,
saying: 'Get down! Be off with all that dog pack!'

And then he ringed both arms around my neck.                 43*
He kissed my face, then said: 'You wrathful soul!
Blessed the one that held you in her womb.

That man, alive, flaunted his arrogance,                     46
and nothing good adorns his memory.
So here his shadow is possessed with rage.

How many, in the world above, pose there                     49
as kings but here will lie like pigs in muck,
leaving behind them horrible dispraise.'

'Sir,' I replied, 'this I should really like:                52
before we make our way beyond this lake,
to see him dabbled in the minestrone.'

He gave me my answer: 'Before that shore                     55
has come to view, you'll surely have your fill.
And rightly you rejoice in this desire.'

Then, moments on, I saw that sinner ripped                   58
to vicious tatters by that mud-caked lot.
I praise God still, and still give thanks for that.

'Get him,' they howled. 'Let's get him – Silver Phil!'       61
That crazy Florentine! He bucked, he baulked.
Turning, the Guelf turned teeth upon himself.

64     We left him there. Of him, my story tells no more.
And yet my ears were pierced with cries of pain.
At which, I barred my eyes intently forwards.

67     'Dear son,' my teacher in his goodness said,
'we now approach the city known as Dis,
its teeming crowds and weighty citizens.'

70     'Already, sir,' I said, 'I clearly can
make out the minarets beyond this moat,
as bright and red, it seems, as if they sprang

73     from fire.' 'Eternal fire,' he answered me,
'burning within, projects, as you can see,
these glowing profiles from the depths of Hell.'

76     We now arrived within the deep-dug ditch –
the channel round that place disconsolate,
whose walls, it seemed to me, were formed of iron.

79     Not without, first, encircling it about,
we came to where the ferry man broke forth:
'Out you all get!' he yelled. 'The entry's here.'

82     I saw there, on that threshold – framed – more than
a thousand who had rained from Heaven. Spitting
in wrath. 'Who's that,' they hissed, 'who, yet undead,

85     travels the kingdom of the truly dead?'
He gave a sign, my teacher in all wisdom,
saying he sought some secret word with them.

88     At which they somewhat hid their fierce disdain.
'You come, but on your own!' they said. 'Let him,
so brazen entering our realm, walk by.

91     He may retrace his foolish path alone –
or try it, if he can – while you'll stay here.
You've been his escort through this dark terrain.'

94     Reader, imagine! I grew faint at heart,
to hear these cursed phrases ringing out.
I truly thought I'd never make it back.

97     'My guide, my dearest master. Seven times –
or more by now – you've brought me safely through.
You've drawn me from the face of towering doom.

Do not, I beg you, leave me here undone.          100
If we are now denied a clear way on,
then let us quickly trace our footsteps back.'

My lord had led me onwards to that place –        103
and now he said: 'Do not be terrified.
No one can take from us our right to pass.

Wait here a while. Refresh your weary soul.       106
Take strength. Be comforted. Feed on good hope.
I'll not desert you in this nether world.'

So off he went. He there abandoned me,            109
my sweetest father. Plunged in 'perhapses',
I so remained, brain arguing 'yes' and 'no'.

What he then said to them I could not tell.       112
Yet hardly had he taken up his stand
when all ran, jostling, to return inside.

They barred the door, these enemies of ours,      115
to meet his thrust. My lord remained shut out.
With heavy tread, he now came back to me.

Eyes bent upon the ground, his forehead shaved    118
of all brave confidence, sighing, he said:
'Who dares deny me entrance to this house of grief?'

To me he said: 'You see. I'm angry now.           121
Don't be dismayed. They'll fuss around in there.
They'll seek to keep us out. But I'll win through.

This insolence of theirs is nothing new.          124*
At some less secret gate they tried it once.
But that still stands without its lock, ajar.

You've seen the door, dead words scribed on its beam.  127
And now already there descends the slope –
passing these circles, and without a guide –
    someone through whom the city will lie open.'       130

# CANTO 9

1      The colour that courage failing brought out
so quickly in me, seeing my leader retreat,
made him, the sooner, check his own new pallor.

4      Intently, as though listening hard, he stopped.
Eyesight unaided – in that blackened air,
through foggy, dense swirls – could not carry far.

7*      'This contest, even so, we're bound to win.
If not . . .' he began. 'Yet granted such a one . . .
How long to me it seems till that one comes!'

10      I saw quite clearly how he covered up
his opening thoughts with those that followed on –
words inconsistent with the first he spoke.

13      Yet fear came over me at what he had said.
And so, from these truncated words, I drew
a meaning worse, perhaps, than he had meant.

16      'Into the hollow deep of this grim bowl
do any make their way from that first rung
where nothing, save for thwarted hope, brings pain?'

19      I put this question to him. 'Seldom,' he said.
'It happens rarely that our people take
the path that I am venturing to tread.

22*      It's true, of course, I've been here once before,
conjured to come by bitter Erichtho –
she who called shadows back into their limbs.

25      A short while only was I bare of flesh
until, as she compelled, I breached these walls
to fetch a spirit from the Judas ring.

That is the utmost deep, the darkest place,                28
the furthest from the sky's all-turning sphere.
I know the way. Be confident, be sure.

    This marsh, exhaling such a nauseous stench,      31
forms in a belt around the mournful town
and not without due anger shall we enter in.'

    He said much more. But what I can't recall.       34
My eyes in all attention now were drawn
towards the blazing summit of that gate,

    where suddenly, at one point, there had sprung   37*
three blood-stained Furies from the depths of Hell.
In pose and body they were, all three, women,

    wound round about with water snakes, bright green.   40
Fringing their vicious brows they bore, as hair,
entwining snakes. Their curls were sharp-horned vipers.

    And he – who knew quite well that these were slaves   43
who served the empress of unending tears –
said to me: 'Look! The cruel Eumenides!

    That one's Megaera, on the left-hand side.        46
Weeping there stands Alecto, on the right.
Tisiphone's between these two.' He paused.

    Each rent her breast with her own fingernails.    49
With slapping palm, each beat herself and screamed –
so loud I strained, all doubt, against the poet.

    'Come now, Medusa! Turn him – quick! – to stone!'   52*
Staring hard down they spoke in unison.
'The Theseus raid went unavenged! We're wrong!'

    'Turn round! Your back to them! Your eyes tight shut!   55
For if the Gorgon shows and you catch sight,
there'll be no way of ever getting out.'

    He spoke and then, himself, he made me turn       58
and, not relying on my hands alone,
to shield my eyes he closed his own on mine.

    Look hard, all you whose minds are sound and sane,   61
and wonder at the meaning lying veiled
beyond the curtain of this alien verse.

64      Already across the turbid swell there came
a shattering resonance that, charged with panic,
evoked great tremors down each river bank.

67      In this way, too, a driving wind – impelled
by clashing currents through the burning air –
strikes at a grove and, meeting no resistance,

70      splinters the branches flat and bears them off.
So, proudly on it goes, in clouds of dust,
shepherds and beasts all fleeing in its path.

73      He loosed my eyes, 'And now,' he said, 'stretch straight
your strings of sight across this age-old scum
to where the fumes are thickest, stinging most.'

76      Like frogs that glimpse their enemy the snake,
and vanish rapidly across the pond –
diving till each sits huddling on its bed –

79      I saw a thousand ruined souls or more
scattering in flight, ahead of one whose pace
passed, yet kept dry, across the river Styx.

82      The greasy air he wafted from his face,
his left hand drawn before him, as a fan.
And this was all the strain, it seemed, that tired him.

85      I saw full well that he was sent from Heaven,
I turned towards my teacher, and he signed
that I should bend in silent deference.

88      How full he seemed to me of high disdain!
He reached the gates. And, simply with his rod,
he opened them. For nothing held them firm.

91      'Outcasts from Heaven, driven beyond contempt!'
Thus, in that dreadful doorway, he began:
'How is such truculence bred up in you?

94      Why so recalcitrant against that will
whose aim and purpose never can be maimed,
which has so often now increased your pain?

97*      What is the point? Why kick against your fate?
Your guard dog Cerberus is still (remember?)
hairless for doing so, at chin and neck.'

He then turned back along the filthy road.  100
He spoke no word to us. He had the look
of someone gnawed and gathered up by care –
　　though not the cares that here confronted him.  103
And now we set our tread towards that land.
The holy words had made us confident.
　　We entered. And no force was offered us.  106
So, eager to survey what such a fort
could lock within the confines of its wall,
　　when once inside, I cast my eyes about.  109
I see a plain, extending all around.
And everywhere is grief and wracking pain.
　　Compare: at Arles (the Rhône there forms a marsh),  112*
or else at Polj by the Kvarner gulf,
which shuts the door on Italy and bathes its bounds,
　　are sepulchres that make the ground uneven.  115
And so, too, here, a tomb at every turn,
except that all was done more bitterly.
　　For flames were scattered round among these tombs.  118
The pits were therefore so intensely fired,
no tradesman needs his brand iron half so hot.
　　The covers of the tombs all stood half-raised;  121
and out of each there came such cruel lamenting
these must have been the cries from pain within.
　　And I to my master: 'Who can these all be,  124
these people buried in the sepulchres?
They make their presence felt in such pained sighs?'
　　The answer: 'These are the master heretics,  127
with all their followers from every sect.
These tombs are filled with more than you suspect.
　　Those of like mind are buried each with each.  130
The monuments are all at differing heats.'
He turned towards the right, then on we went,
　　between the torments and high battlements.  133

# CANTO 10

1    Onward along a secret path – confined
between those ramparts and the shows of pain –
my teacher led and I was at his shoulder.

4    'You,' I began, 'true power and height of strength,
you bring me, turning, through these godless whirls.
Speak, if this pleases you. Feed my desires.

7    Those people lying in the sepulchres –
what chance is there of seeing them? The lids
are off already. No one stands on guard.'

10*   'These tombs,' he said, 'will finally be shut
when, from Jehoshaphat on Judgement Day,
sinners bring back their bodies left above.

13*   This circle is the cemetery for all
disciples of the Epicurus school,
who say the body dies, so too the soul.

16   The question, therefore, that you've put to me,
once you're within, will soon be satisfied,
so, too, the longing that you keep unsaid.'

19   'I never would – my lord, my trusted guide –
keep, save for brevity, my heart from you.
And brevity you've urged on me before.'

22*   'Tuscan! You go through the city of fire
alive and speaking as a man of worth.
Come, if you will, and rest in this domain.

25   Your accent manifests that you were born
a son of that great fatherland on which,
perhaps, I wreaked too harsh an injury.'

This sound, so suddenly, came ringing out 28
from one among the sepulchres. Fearful,
I shrank still closer to my leader's side.

'What's wrong?' he said to me. 'Just turn around! 31*
And see there, upright, risen, Farinata.
From cincture upwards you will see him whole.'

My gaze was trained already into his, 34
while he, brow raised, was thrusting out his chest,
as though he held all Hell in high disdain.

My leader (hands in animated aid) 37
drove me towards him down the line of vaults.
He counselled: 'Let your words be duly measured.'

So there, beneath his sepulchre, I stood. 40
He looked me up and down a while, and then
inquired, half-scornfully: 'Who were your forebears?'

I – always eager and obedient – 43
concealing nothing, laid all plainly forth.
At which he arched his brows a little more.

And then: 'In fierce hostility, they stood 46
against myself, my ancestors, my cause.
And so, on two occasions, they were scattered wide.'

'Scattered,' I answered, 'so they may have been, 49
but all came back from all sides, then and now.
And your men truly never learned that art.'

Then there arose, revealed before my eyes, 52*
a shadow near the first, seen from chin up,
which had, as I suppose, just risen to its knees.

It looked me all around, as though intent 55
on seeing whether, with me, was another.
But when its doubting glance was wholly spent,

weeping he called: 'If you, through this eyeless 58
prison, pass on through height of intellect,
my son, where is he? And why not here with you?'

'I come,' I said, 'though not through my own strength. 61
The man who waits there leads me through this place
to one, perhaps, whom once your Guido scorned.'

64  The way he spoke – and what he suffered, too –
had now already spelled for me his name.
And that was why my answer was so full.

67*  Upright suddenly: 'What's that you say?'
he wailed. '"He once . . ."? You mean, he's not alive?
And are his eyes not struck by bonny light?'

70  But then, in noticing that slight delay
which came before I offered my reply,
he fell back flat, and did not re-appear.

73  The other noble soul (at whose command
I'd come to rest) in no way changed expression.
He neither moved his neck nor bent his waist.

76*  But still continuing in what he'd said:
'If,' he went on, 'they learned that art so ill,
that is more torment than this bed of pain.

79  And yet no more than fifty times that face
(the moon's, who is our sovereign here) will shine
till you shall learn how heavy that art weighs.

82  If you once more would gain the lovely world,
tell me: how dare those burghers, in their laws,
oppose themselves so viciously to mine?'

85  My answer was: 'The massacre, the mindless waste
that stained the flowing Arbia with blood,
led, in our oratories, to these demands.'

88  Sighing, he did now move his head. 'In none
of that,' he said, 'was I alone. And I
would not, without good cause, have gone with them.

91  I was alone – where all the rest could bear
to think that Florence might be swept away –
and boldly stood to speak in her defence.'

94  'Well (may your seed find sometime true repose!)
untie the knot for me,' I now besought,
'so tightly twined around my searching thoughts.

97*  You see, it seems (to judge from what I hear)
far in advance what time will bring to pass,
but otherwise in terms of present things.'

'We see like those who suffer from ill light.                    100
We are,' he said, 'aware of distant things.
Thus far He shines in us, the Lord on high.

But when a thing draws near to us, our minds          103
go blank. So if no other brings us news,
then nothing of your human state is known to us.

You will from this be able to deduce                       106
that all our knowledge will be wholly dead
when all the doors of future time are closed.'

And then I said, as though my heart were pierced        109
with guilt, 'Go, say to him, that fallen soul,
his first-born son is still among the living.

And if, before I answered, I fell mute,                      112
I did so (make him understand) because
my thoughts – which you have solved – had strayed to
       doubt.'

By now, my teacher had already called.                    115
And so, with greater urgency I begged that soul
that he should tell me who was with him there.

'I lie,' he answered, 'with a thousand, more.            118*
Enclosed beside me is the second Frederick.
Cardinal Octavian, too. Of others, I keep silent.'

And then he hid: and I, towards that great               121
poet of the ancient world, turned my steps backwards,
musing on words that seemed my enemy.

He went his way and, as he walked, he asked:           124
'Why is it you're so lost in thought, so blurred by doubt?'
And I responded fully to his words.

'Keep well in mind,' my lord in wisdom said,           127
'the things that you have heard against yourself.
But now,' his finger raised, 'attend to this:

when once again you stand within the rays              130*
that she, whose lovely eyes see all things, casts,
you'll learn from her what your life's course will be.'

133     And then he swung, to tread towards the left.
We quit the wall and headed for the middle.
The path we took cut straight into a gorge,
136         and even from above the stench was foul.

# CANTO 11

Now near the brink of a sheer escarpment    1
formed in a circle from great, shattered stones,
we found, below, a crueller bunch of souls.

And there, against an awful overflow –    4
a stink arising from the utmost depths –
we huddled back together by the lid

of one vast sepulchre, inscribed, I saw,    7*
in words that said: 'I guard Pope Anastasius,
drawn by Photinus from the rightful road.'

'Best not descend too rapidly, but first    10
get more accustomed in our sense of smell
to this grim belch. We'll then not notice it.'

These were my teacher's words. To him I said,    13
'Find something that will compensate, to waste
no time.' 'I'm thinking, as you see,' he said,

and then began: 'Dear son, within this rock-rimmed pit    16
three lesser circuits lie. And these (like those
you leave behind) go down by due degrees.

Each rung is crammed with spirits of the damned.    19*
But listen now – so sight may henceforth serve –
and hear the "what" and "why" of their constraints.

Malice is aimed in all its forms – and thus    22*
incurs the hatred of Heaven – at gross injustice,
and, aiming so, harms others, by deceit or force.

Deceit, though, is specifically a human wrong,    25*
and hence displeases God the more. Liars
are therefore deeper down, and tortured worse.

48

Ring One throughout is meant for violent wills.
But violent acts may fall upon three persons.
And so this ring is shaped and formed in three.

31     To God, to self, to neighbours hurt is done
(to persons, of course, but also their possessions)
in ways that you will now hear argued out.

34     To those around us, death or grievous wounds
are wrought by violent hands, the things we own
ruined by outrage, extortion or fire.

37     So in the agonies of Sub-ring One,
in different squads, are homicides and thugs,
vandals and looters, bandits and brigands.

40     In violence, too, we turn against ourselves,
or else our own belongings. And thus
in Sub-ring Two are those (regret now vain)

43     who by their own free will strips off your world
or gambles all their competence away,
and weeps where, properly, they should rejoice.

46     Force, too, is offered to the Deity
by hearts, blaspheming, that deny His power,
or else scorn Nature and her great largesse.

49*    And so the imprint of the smallest ring
falls on Cahorsian bankers, as on Sodom,
and those who speak at heart in scorn of God.

52*    As for deceit – which gnaws all rational minds –
we practise this on those who trust in us,
or those whose pockets have no room for trust.

55     Fraud of the second kind will only gash
the ligature of love that Nature forms:
and therefore in great Circle Two there nests

58     smarm and hypocrisy, the casting-up of spells,
impersonation, thievery, crooked priests,
embezzlement and pimping, such-like scum.

61     Fraud of the other sort forgets no less
the love that Nature makes, but then, as well,
the love particular that trust creates.

So in the smallest ring of all – that point        64
within the universe where Satan sits –
consumed eternally, are traitors, every one.

'Your explanation, sir,' I said, 'proceeds        67
with great lucidity. You clarify
the levels of this grim abyss and all within.

Yet tell me, too: those souls in that gross marsh,        70
those swept by winds, those creatures lashed by rain,
and those that clash with such abrasive tongues,

if they all, likewise, face the wrath of God,        73
then why not racked within these flame-red walls?
Or if they don't, why are they as they are?'

'Why,' he replied, 'do your frenetic wits        76*
wander so wildly from their usual track?
Or where, if not fixed here, are your thoughts set?

Do you, at any rate, not call to mind        79
the terms in which your *Ethics* fully treats
those three dispositions that the Heavens repel:

intemperance, intentional harm and mad        82
brutality? Or that intemperance
offends God least, and least attracts His blame?

If you think carefully of what this means,        85
and summon into thought what those souls are
who serve their sentence in the upper ring,

you'll plainly see why these are set apart        88
from those condemned as felons, and, in pain,
less sharply hammered by divine revenge.'

'You are the sun who heals all clouded sight.        91
Solving my doubts, you bring me such content
that doubt, no less than knowing, is delight.

But still,' I said, 'turn backwards to the point        94*
where you declared that usury offends
God's generosity. Untie that knot.'

'Philosophy, as those that read it know,        97
takes note,' he said, 'on more than one occasion,
of how the course that Nature runs is drawn

100      directly from the mind and art of God.
And if you read your *Physics* with due care,
you'll see, before you're many pages through,

103      that your art takes, as best it can, the lead
that Nature gives – as student does from master.
Your art is nearly grandchild, then, to God.

106      From these two principles – if you recall
the opening lines of Genesis – we're bound to draw
our living strength and multiply our people.

109      But usurers adopt a different course.
They place their hopes in other things, and thus
make mock of Nature's self and her close kin.

112*      But follow on. I'm ready now to go.
The writhing Fish have swum to the horizon.
The Wain lies high above the Western Wind.

115      The leap we now must make lies far beyond.'

# CANTO 12

The place we'd reached – to clamber down that bank –     1
was alpine crag. No eye, considering
what else was there, would not have flinched away.

Compare: an avalanche in Adige,     4*
southwards of Trent, once struck the mountain flank,
triggered perhaps by landslip or earthquake;

and boulders from the summit shifted down     7
in steps and stages to the valley floor,
to offer those up there a downward route.

Likewise the path we trod down this ravine.     10*
And on the angle where the incline broke,
there lay stretched out the infamy of Crete,

spawned in the womb of Pasiphae's fake heifer.     13
And when he saw us there he gnawed himself,
as though flailed flat within by utter rage.

My leader in his wisdom called towards him:     16
'You may suppose that he's the duke of Athens,
who dealt you, in the world above, your death.

You monster! Move aside! This one's not come     19
provided with instructions from your sister.
He comes to see what you are suffering here.'

A stunned bull, stricken by its mortal blow,     22
wrenches, that instant, free from noose and rope.
It cannot walk but skips and hops about.

The Minotaur, I saw, behaved like that.     25
'Run!' shouted Virgil, watching out. 'A gap!
Better get down while still his fury bites.'

28    So down across the scree we picked our way.
      Beneath my feet, the stones would often move,
      teetering beneath the strange new weight they bore.

31*   I walked on, deep in thought. 'Perhaps,' he said,
      'you're thinking of this landslide? Or that guard
      whose brutal anger I have just eclipsed?

34    When once before (I'd like you now to know)
      I came down here and entered lower Hell,
      these cliffs had yet to suffer any rock fall.

37    But certainly, if I have got this right,
      there once came One who gathered up from Dis
      the stolen treasure of its highest place.

40    Moments before, a tremor in every part
      disturbed these fetid depths. The universe
      must then, I think, have felt that love through which

43    it often turns (so some suppose) to chaos.
      At that same point, these age-old crags were rent
      and left both here and elsewhere as they are.

46    But fix your eyes upon the valley floor.
      We now are nearing the river of blood.
      There simmer all whose violence damaged others.'

49    What blind cupidity, what crazy rage
      impels us onwards in our little lives –
      then dunks us in this stew to all eternity!

52    I saw there (as my guide had said I would)
      a ditch of great dimensions in an arc
      that stretched its wide embrace around the plain.

55*   And there, between the hill foot and those banks,
      were centaurs, running in a long-drawn line,
      armed – as they'd been on earth to hunt – with arrows.

58    On seeing us descend, they all reined in.
      Three of that company then sallied forth,
      their barbs and bow strings already well picked.

61    And one, still distant, shouted out: 'What pain
      have you to meet, now making down that butte?
      Tell us from there. Or else I draw my bow.'

My teacher in response then said: 'To Chiron –          64
there, just beside you – we shall make reply.
You are too headstrong. And you always were.'

'That's Nessus there,' he said, alerting me.          67
'He died for love of lovely Deianira,
but then avenged himself with his own blood.

The middle one (eyes fixed upon his chest)          70
is Chiron the Great. He nurtured Achilles.
Pholus, who lived so full of wrath, is third.

Around this ditch, in thousands these all run,          73
and loose their arrows at those souls that strain
higher beyond the blood than guilt allows.'

We drew now closer to those swift-foot beasts.          76
Then Chiron plucked a shaft and, with its notch,
he combed his beard and tucked it from his jaw.

And, once he'd made his noble mouth thus free,          79
he said to his companions: 'Have you seen
the one behind, how all he touches moves?

A normal dead man's feet would not do that.'          82
My trusted leader was now standing where,
around the waist, the double nature weds.

He answered thus: 'He is indeed alive.          85
To me it falls to show him this dark vale.
Necessity, not pleasure, leads us on.

Someone whose hymn is the "Alleluia"          88*
paused in that song to hand me this new task.
He is no robber, I no thievish soul.

Now in the name of that True Power by which          91
I move each step along this tangled way,
allot a guide to us from your own band

to show us where the ford might be, and bear          94
this man beside me on his crupper.'
He is no spirit walking through the air.

Now Chiron turned, to pivot to his right.          97
'Go back!' he said to Nessus. 'Be their guide.
Make any troop you stumble on give way.'

100     The escort by our side, we now moved on
along the shore of boiling vermilion
where souls, well boiled, gave vent to high-pitched yells.

103     Some, so I saw, were plunged there to the brow.
'And these,' the mighty centaur said, 'are tyrants.
They lent their hands to violent gain and blood.

106*     So here, in tears for their unpitying sins,
with Alexander there is vicious Dionysius,
who brought on Sicily such grieving years.

109     That forehead there – its quiff as black as jet –
is Azzolino. At his side the blond
Opizzo d'Este, who – and this is true –

112     was done to death by his own bastard son.'
I turned towards the poet, who now said:
'Let him go first and I'll be next to come.'

115     A little further on, the centaur stopped,
arched over people who emerged, it seemed,
throat high above the seething of that stream.

118     There, to one side, he pointed out a shade.
'He stabbed,' he said, 'in the bosom of God,
the one whose heart drips blood still on the Thames.'

121     I now saw some with heads above the flood,
then others further on, their torsos clear.
And these, in greater numbers, I could recognize.

124     Then, gradually, the blood race grew more shallow –
so that by now it only stewed their toes.
And there we found the crossing of the ditch.

127     'On this side – see? – the boiling stream grows less.
So, correspondingly,' the centaur said,
'I'd have you understand that, over there,

130     the bed is pressed, in process point by point,
still further down until it finds the place
at which in pain great despots wring out moans.

133     Justice divine on that side sharply stings
the hun Attila – scourge of all the earth –
Pyrrhus and Sextus. There it also milks

the tears eternally that boiling wave unlocks 136
from Renier the Mad to Renier da Corneto,
who wrought such strife upon the open roads.'
 And then he turned and passed the ford once more. 139

# CANTO 13

1      No, Nessus had not reached the other side
       when we began to travel through a wood
       that bore no sign of any path ahead.

4      No fresh green leaves but murky in colour,
       no boughs clean arc-ed but knotty and entwined,
       no apples were there but thorns, poison-pricked.

7*     No scrubby wilderness so bitter and dense
       from Cécina as far as Corneto
       offers a den to beasts that hate ploughed farmlands.

10     Their nest is there, those disgusting Harpies
       who drove the Trojans from the Strophades,
       with grim announcements of great harm to come.

13     Wings widespreading, human from neck to brow,
       talons for feet, plumage around their paunches,
       they sing from these uncanny trees their songs of woe.

16     Constant in kindness, my teacher now said:
       'Before you venture further in, please know
       that you now stand in Sub-ring Number Two,

19     and shall until you reach the Appalling Sands.
       So look around. Take care. What you'll see here
       would drain belief from any word I uttered.'

22     A wailing I heard, dragged out from every part,
       and saw there no one who might make these sounds,
       so that I stopped, bewildered, in my tracks.

25*    Truly I think he truly thought that, truly,
       I might have, just, believed these voices rose
       from persons hiding from us in the thorn maze.

Therefore: 'If you,' my teacher said, 'will wrench        28
away some sprig from any tree you choose,
that will lop short your feeling in such doubt.'

And so I reached my hand a little forwards.        31*
I plucked a shoot (no more) from one great hawthorn.
At which its trunk screamed out: 'Why splinter me?'

Now darkened by a flow of blood, the tree        34
spoke out a second time: 'Why gash me so?
Is there no living pity in your heart?

Once we were men. We've now become dry sticks.        37
Your hand might well have proved more merciful
if we had been the hissing souls of snakes.'

Compare: a green brand, kindled at one end –        40
the other oozing sap – whistles and spits
as air finds vent, then rushes out as wind.

So now there ran, out of this fractured spigot,        43
both words and blood. At which I let the tip
drop down and stood like someone terror-struck.

'You injured soul!' my teacher (sane as ever)        46
answered. 'If he had only earlier
believed what my own writings could have shown,

he'd not have stretched his hand so far towards you.        49
This, though, is all beyond belief. So I was forced
to urge a deed that presses on my own mind still.

But tell him now who once you were. He may,        52
in turn, as remedy, refresh your fame,
returning to the world above by leave.'

The trunk: 'Your words, sir, prove so sweet a bait,        55
I cannot here keep silence. Don't be irked
if I a while should settle on that lure and talk.

I am the one who held in hand both keys        58
to Federigo's heart. I turned them there,
locking so smoothly and unlocking it

that all men, almost, I stole from his secrets.        61
Faith I kept, so true in that proud office
I wasted sleep and lost my steady pulse.

64    That harlot Scandal, then (her raddled eyes
she never drags from where the emperor dwells,
the vice of court life, mortal blight of all)

67    enflamed the minds of everyone against me.
And they in flames enflamed the great Augustus.
So, happy honours turned to hapless grief.

70    My mind – itself disdainful in its tastes –
believing it could flee disdain by dying,
made me unjust against myself so just.

73    By all these weird, new-wooded roots, I swear
on oath before you: I did not break faith,
nor failed a lord so worthy of regard.

76    Will you – should either head back to the world –
bring comfort to my memory, which lies
still lashed beneath the stroke of envious eyes?'

79    Pausing a while, he said (my chosen poet),
'He's silent now, so waste no opportunity.
If there is more you wish to know, then say.'

82    'You,' I replied, 'must speak once more and ask
what you believe will leave me satisfied.
I could not do it. Pity wrings my core.'

85    And so he did once more begin: 'Suppose
that freely, from a generous heart, someone
should do, imprisoned ghost, what your prayers seek,

88    tell us, if you should care to, this: how souls
are bound in these hard knots. And, if you can:
will anyone be ever loosed from limbs like these?'

91    At that (exhaling heavily) the trunk
converted wind to word and formed this speech:
'The answer you require is quick to give:

94    When any soul abandons savagely
its body, rending self by self away,
Minos consigns it to the seventh gulf.

97    Falling, it finds this copse. Yet no one place
is chosen as its plot. Where fortune slings it,
there (as spelt grains might) it germinates.

A sapling sprouts, grows ligneous, and then        100
the Harpies, grazing on its foliage,
fashion sharp pain and windows for that pain.

  We (as shall all), come Judgement Day, shall seek     103
our cast-off spoil, yet not put on this vestment.
Keeping what we tore off would not be fair.

  Our bodies we shall drag back here; and all        106*
around this melancholy grove they'll swing,
each on the thorn of shades that wrought them harm.'

  Attention trained entirely on that stock        109
(thinking, in truth, it might as yet say more),
we now were shocked by a sudden uproar,

  as if (to make comparison) you'd heard some hog    112
and all the boar hunt baying round its stand –
a sound composed of beasts and thrashing twigs.

  And look there, on the left-hand side, there came,   115*
at speed, two fleeing, naked, scratched to bits,
who broke down every hurdle in that scrub.

  One was ahead: 'Quick, quick! Come, death! Come
      now!'        118
The other (seeming, to himself, too slow)
was yelling: 'Lano! Oh, your nimble heels

  weren't half so nifty at the Toppo rumble!'    121
And then (it may be his breath was failing),
he sank to form a clump beside a shrub.

  Behind these two, the wood was teeming, full    124
of black bitches, ravenous and rapid,
as greyhounds are when slipping from their leads.

  These set their teeth on that sad, hunkered form.   127
They tore him all to pieces, chunk by chunk.
And then they carried off those suffering limbs.

  My guide then took me gently by the hand,      130
and led me to the bush, which wept (in vain)
through all of its blood-stained lacerations,

  saying: 'O Jacopo da Santo Andrea!      133
What use was it to take me as your shield?
Am I to blame for your wild, wicked ways?'

136     My teacher came and stood above that bush.
'So who were you,' he said, 'who, pierced to bits,
breathes painful utterance in jets of blood?'

139     'You souls,' he said, 'you come – but just in time –
to see the massacre, in all its shame,
that rends away from me my fresh green fronds.

142*     Place all these leaves beneath this grieving stump.
I too was from that city, once, which chose
Saint John as patron over Mars – its first –

145     whose arts, since spurned, have always brought us harm.
And were there not, beneath the Arno bridge,
some traces visible of what he was,

148     those citizens who built it all anew
on ashes that Attila left behind
would then have laboured with no end in view.

151     Myself, I made a gallows of my house.'

# CANTO 14

Seized, in pure charity, by love of home,                    1
I gathered up those scattered leaves, then bore them
towards my countryman, his voice grown dim.

And then, from there, we reached the boundary             4
of circuits two and three and witnessed now,
in horror and awe, how skilful justice is.

To make more manifest what now was new,                    7
we'd reached, I'd better say, an open plain
that dusts all vegetation from its floor.

Round this, the wood of pain creates a fringe             10
(as likewise, round that wood, the wretched ditch).
And here we halted at the very edge.

The ground beneath was brushed with coarse, dry sand,  13*
no different from those arid Libyan wastes
on which the feet of Cato marched to war.

Great God! Your vengeance must be rightly feared          16
by all who read the verses I compose
to say what there was straight before my eyes.

I saw ahead a flock of naked souls.                       19
And all were weeping, very mournfully.
But each was subject to a different law.

Some of these folk lay supine on the ground,             22
and some sat huddling, tight about themselves.
Others again strode endlessly around.

The latter were, in number, far the more.                 25
Those lying flat, though fewer, were in tongue
more free at voicing their sharp miseries.

28　　　And over all that barren sand there fell –
　　　as slow as Alpine snow on windless days –
　　　a shower of broad-winged fire flakes drifting down.

31*　　Recall how Alexander, on his march
　　　across the climes of scorching India,
　　　saw clouds of fire that fell around his troops

34　　　and reached the earth still whole. He therefore made
　　　his squadrons stamp the ground, since, broken down,
　　　these vapours proved far easier to quell.

37　　　So, too, eternally, the flames fell here.
　　　The sand caught fire, like tinder under flint,
　　　and doubled – from beneath – the upper punishment.

40　　　Unrestingly, their wretched hands jived on –
　　　now up, now down, now high, now low, slap, clap! –
　　　to shake fresh drops of ardour from their skin.

43　　　So I began: 'You, sir, in everything
　　　have conquered all, though not those demons, hard-faced,
　　　at the gate of Dis, who stopped us on that step.

46*　　That hero there, who's he? Heedless he seems
　　　of these incendiaries. Scowling in scorn,
　　　it seems he lies unripened by the rain.'

49　　　The man himself roared forth (for he had seen
　　　that I, in questioning my lord, meant him):
　　　'What I, once living, was, so dead I am.

52　　　Yes! Jupiter may tire the blacksmith out
　　　from whom he tore in wrath the thunder spear
　　　by which I stood, on my last day, drilled through;

55*　　and others, too, he may exhaust, in shifts
　　　that stoke that black forge under Mount Jabal,
　　　bellowing: "Vulcan! Aid, more aid! Good man!"

58　　　just as he did when battle raged at Flegra,
　　　and loose his bolts at me with all his force . . .
　　　But no! No sweet revenge he'd have on me!'

61　　　My leader then spoke out with greater strength
　　　than ever I, till then, had heard him use:
　　　'Oh, Capaneus! Pride yet uninterred!

This punishment, in consequence, is yours.   64
No agony, except your own great rage,
would serve as proper answer to your ire.'

And then – a better look around his lips –   67
he turned to me. 'This man,' he said, 'a king,
was one of seven laying siege to Thebes.

God he disdained – he seems to, still – and seemed   70
to pay Him scant regard. So, as I said:
disdain alone must be his sole medallion.

And now keep close behind. Take every care.   73
Do not set foot upon these blistering sands.
Follow the wood's verge round at every step.'

In silence now, continuing, we came   76
to where a rill flows spurting from the grove.
Remembering its redness, I still squirm.

As in Viterbo there's the Bubble Brook –   79*
which scarlet women, bathing, share between them –
so this stream took its course across the sand.

That rivulet, in bed and bank, was formed   82
of stone, as also were the margins by its side.
This, I could tell, was where our best path lay.

'Among so many other things that I –   85
since entering the gate through which
no foot is ever disallowed an entry –

have shown to you, nothing your eyes have spied   88
has been more notable than this stream here,
above which all the sparks grow dim and die.'

These were the words my leader spoke to me.   91
And I besought him, through his great largesse,
to grant the food in granting me the hunger.

'Mid-sea,' he said, 'there lies a land now waste.   94*
To us, this land is known as Crete, where once,
when Saturn ruled as king, the world was chaste.

A mountain stands there, Idaeus its name.   97
This, once, rejoiced in streams and leafy fronds,
but now stands abandoned like forbidden ground.

100    Once, Rhea – seeking for a sanctuary –
       chose here to lay her boy child, Jove. And then,
       to hide his wailings, called for dance and din.

103    Within those caves an aged man stands tall.
       His back is turned to Egypt and Damiatta.
       Rome is the mirror into which he stares.

106    His head is modelled in the finest gold.
       Of purest silver are his arms and breast.
       Then downwards to the fork he's brightest brass,

109    and all below is iron of choicest ore.
       The right foot, though, is formed of terracotta.
       On that he puts more weight than on the left.

112    And every part that is not gold is cracked.
       Tears through this single fissure drizzle down,
       then, mingling, penetrate the cavern wall.

115    Their rocky course cascades to this deep hollow.
       They form the Acheron, Styx and Phlegethon.
       These then disgorge themselves through this tight race,

118    until (since there is no way further on)
       they all collect as Cocytus. But you yourself
       will see that pool. So I'll not tell the tale.'

121    'If,' I now put to him, 'this gutter flows
       from somewhere in our human world, then why
       do we just see it at this selvage hem?'

124    'You know,' he said, 'this place is circular.
       Yet, far as you have sunk in your descent,
       your path has always tended to the left.

127    So you have still not spanned the circle round;
       and if new things now show themselves to us,
       it should not stir amazement on your brow.'

130    And I kept on at him: 'And so, sire, where
       are Phlegethon and Lethe found? The one, you say,
       rains down in tears. The other you are silent of.'

133    'By everything you ask,' he said, 'I'm pleased.
       And yet, as one solution, you should note
       the seething redness of the waters here.

Lethe you'll see, but far beyond this ditch.                    136
Its waves are where the soul will go to wash,
when guilt, repented, is at last removed.'

    And then: 'It's time for you to leave this wood.          139
So come. Keep close behind me as you do.
The banks, which are not burned, provide a road.

    These vapours are extinguished over it.'                  142

# CANTO 15

| 1 | We're carried down by one of those hard shores, |
| | while vapours from the brook rise, arching up, |
| | to save both stream and margins from the fire. |
| 4 | Flemings, enflamed – from Wissant on to Bruges – |
| | in terror of the floods that blast towards them, |
| | construct great screens to put the sea to flight. |
| 7 | So, too, the Paduans, along the Brent, |
| | attempt to shield their castles and estates, |
| | before its source (Carinthia) is touched by heat. |
| 10 | Modelled on some original like these |
| | (whatever master hand contrived them so) |
| | these breaks were formed, though not that high or broad. |
| 13 | By now, we'd left the grove so far behind |
| | that, even had I turned around to look, |
| | I'd not have glimpsed the tract where it was found. |
| 16 | But here we came across a band of souls |
| | who milled around the ditch and met our tread. |
| | And each one peered at us – as people will |
| 19 | on evenings when the moon is new – their brows |
| | towards us, wrinkled into squinting blades, |
| | like those of some old tailor at his needle. |
| 22* | Eyed up and down so closely by this clan, |
| | I now was recognized, as known, by one |
| | who plucked my hem and cried: 'How marvellous!' |
| 25 | And I – as he then stretched an arm towards me – |
| | fixed eyes so keenly through his fire-baked look |
| | that these singed features could not fend away |

my mind from knowing, truly, who he was.                    28
And, reaching down a hand towards his face,
I answered him: 'Brunetto, sir, are you here?'

'Do not, my dearest son,' he said, 'be vexed,             31
but let Brunetto Latino turn and walk
a while along with you. The troops can run!'

'I pray, sir, to the utmost, do. Or should               34
you wish,' I said, 'I'll sit with you, so long
as this man here agrees. I go with him.'

'Dear boy,' he said, 'if any in this herd                37
should ever pause, he lies a hundred years
powerless to fan these searing fires away.

And so move on. I'll follow at your coat-tails           40
then catch up later with that entourage,
which, as it goes, bewails eternal loss.'

I did not dare climb down to quit the causeway           43
and walk with him on equal terms. But still,
as though in reverence, I kept my head bowed low.

'What chance or destiny,' he then began,                 46
'leads you down here before your final day?
And who is this that shows the way to you?'

'There, up above,' I answered him, 'where life           49
is halcyon, I lost myself – my path all blurred –
in some great deep before my years were full.

Only as dawn rose, yesterday, I turned                   52
aside. Then he – as yet again I turned –
appeared, and guides me on the road back home.'

'If,' so he answered, 'you pursue your star,             55
then doubtless you will reach a glorious goal,
supposing, in the happy life, I knew you well.

And I myself (had not I died too soon),                  58
seeing how kind the Heavens looked on you,
would willingly have helped you in your work.

But that malignant and ungrateful race                   61*
descending *ab antico* from Fiesole
(they still retain the taint of crag and hill)

64        will act, because you act so well, as bitter foes.
That much is logical: no luscious fig
can rightly thrive where small, sour sorbus grows.

67        The world, since ancient times, has known they're blind.
The tribe is grasping, envious and proud.
Keep yourself clean of habits of their kind.

70        Fortune for you reserves such great renown
that both these factions – Black and White – will seek
to set their teeth in you. Keep goats from grass!

73        Well may these cattle from Fiesole
make themselves straw but never touch the sprout
that springs (if any does within their dung)

76        to bring to life the sacred seed of Rome –
of those remaining when that ancient place
became the very home and nest of malice.'

79        'If all,' I said to him, 'that I might ask
were answered, and in full, then you would not
be exiled, as you are, from human nature.

82        Fixed in my thoughts, and working at my heart,
an image of you still endures – a dear, good father –
as, in the world, you were when hour by hour

85        you taught me how a man becomes eternal.
How great my gratitude must be, will show,
while I still live, in all my tongue will tell.

88        I write, as you recount it here, the story
of my future course, and keep your words with others.
A lady, if I come to her, will comment.

91        On this point only I would have you clear:
that I, so long as conscience does not chide,
am well prepared for all that Fortune wills.

94        In what you vouch, my ears hear nothing new.
Let Fortune, therefore, do as Fortune pleases –
whirl at her wheel like yokels at their hoe.'

97        My teacher, who had now turned right-about,
looked back at me and fixed me with his eye.
'Those listen well,' he said, 'who take good note.'

So on I go, speaking with lawyer Brunetto.　　　100
I ask who his companions are, the great
and good, the eminent, and men of note.

'Of some,' he said, 'you're right to want to know.　　103
More laudable of others not to speak.
Our time would be too short for all that din.

But all of them, be sure, were men of learning,　　106*
authorities and dons of world renown,
besmirched, when living, with the self-same sin.

And so, among this dismal crowd, runs Priscian.　　109
D'Accorso, too – the Prof. And if you yearn
to set your eyes on such-like mangy scabs,

you could. That bishop there! The Slave of Slaves　　112
transferred him to Vicenza from the Arno.
He left his muscles, ill-distended, there.

I would say more. Yet further I may not　　115
advance nor any longer talk with you.
I see new smoke there, rising from the sand.

I can't consort with those who now draw near.　　118*
My Treasury – may that commend itself.
In that, I still live on. I ask no more.'

Around he swung. To me he seemed like one　　121*
who, in the fields around Verona, runs
for that fine prize, a length of green festoon.

He seemed to be the one that wins, not loses.　　124

# CANTO 16

1    I stood already where the roar and boom
of waters falling to the next great ring
could now be heard – a rumble like a beehive.

4    But then appeared, together, at the run,
three shadows, swerving from a further squad
of those in rasping torment from the rain.

7    Towards us, as they came, each cried aloud:
'Stop there! To us, it seems, you're dressed like one
who travels from our own degenerate homeland.'

10   No! No! I saw how branded by the bite
of fire their limbs all were. New wounds! Old scars!
This, though mere memory, still brings me pain.

13   My teacher paused, attending to their cries.
And then, his eyes on me, he said: 'Now wait.
We owe to these men here some courtesy.

16   Indeed, were not the nature of this place
to shoot down barbs of fire, then haste (I'd say)
should properly be shown by you, not them.'

19   And so again, as now we came to rest,
they all began the song they'd sung before
and, turning, formed among themselves a wheel.

22   Compare: prize wrestlers, with their bare skin oiled,
circle – until they clash, then punch and gouge –
in search of some advantage, grip or hold.

25   These likewise. As they wheeled around, each fixed
their glances hard on me. And so their necks
turned counter always to the track they trod.

'The misery,' thus one began, 'of these                28
vile sands may render us, and all our prayers,
contemptible, our faces, too, now black and burned.

But let our reputations bend your heart.              31
And who are you – now tell – whose living step,
in perfect safety, scours the paths of Hell?

This man, whose prints my own feet trample on,        34
although he now goes naked, shorn of hair,
was once of higher rank than you'd imagine.

Grandson by birth of our good Gualdrada,              37*
he was, by title, Conte Guido Guerra.
Much he achieved alive with mind and sword.

The other next to him who flails the sand             40
is Lord Tegghiaio of the Aldobrands.
He ought to have more pleased the world in word.

I, in excruciating pain with them,                    43
was Iacopo Rusticucci. And, yes,
it was my wife who did me greatest harm.'

If only I'd had cover from the fire,                  46
I'd willingly have flung myself among them.
(I think my teacher would have suffered this.)

But since, down there, I'd soon have singed and baked,  49
fear got the better of the good intent
that stirred my appetite for their embrace.

So I began: 'Great grief, not scornfulness,           52
to see your state was planted in my heart
(and only slowly will it shed its leaves)

the instant that my lord, in words to me,             55
led all my inner thoughts to understand
that persons such as you might soon come by.

I am of your place, too. So, I have heard –           58
and always with affection have proclaimed –
the deeds you've done and honour of your name.

I now take leave of galling fruits, to seek           61
sweet apples, promised by my lord in truth,
but first must reach the centre of the circle.'

64     'Long may your soul lead forth your living limbs!'
       So, in reply, said one of them. 'And – grant
       your fame may long shine after you! – then say:

67       do courtesy and valour dwell, as once
       they did, within the circuit of our city walls?
       Or have they utterly departed thence?

70*      Report of this, from courtly Borsiere
       (who only joined us here of late, and goes
       with our companions there), has caused us pain.'

73       'That race of newly rich, and rapid gains,
       these seeds, Fiorenza, bring to flower in you
       excess and pride. And you already weep for that.'

76       With head thrown back, I cried this, all aloud,
       and they, the three (accepting this response),
       glanced each to each like those who've heard plain truth.

79       'If at so little cost,' they said, 'you speak
       so well and satisfy what others seek,
       then you may happily pronounce at will.

82       And so, should you escape from these dark haunts,
       and go once more to see the lovely stars,
       when you, with pleasure, say that "I was there",

85        then do, we beg you, speak of us to others.'
       With this they broke their wheel and, as they fled,
       their agile limbs in flight were quick as wings.

88       No 'amen' ever was so swiftly said
       as these three disappeared before our eyes.
       And now my teacher thought that we could leave.

91       I came behind. But now, not travelling far,
       the sound of the water was so near at hand
       that we could scarcely hear each other speak.

94*      Compare: a river, near its native source,
       runs through the eastern Apennines due east,
       and first descends the slopes of Monte Viso.

97       Its tranquil name up there is Acqua Cheta.
       But then, on flowing to its lower bed,
       at Forlì it assumes a different mode,

and thunders here, in one great bound, above      100
the Alp Saint Benedict, where – were it eased
from ledge to ledge – the height would need a thousand.

So, likewise, down through one great shattered force,      103
we found, resounding there, a blackened stream –
the din of which would soon have stunned our ears.

Around my waist I wore a braided cord,      106*
and had on past occasion thought, by this,
to snare the leopard with its painted hide.

My leader told me I should slip this off.      109
And when I'd got it wound from round my waist,
I handed it across in twisted knots.

And then he turned towards his right-hand side,      112
and flung it, bunched, some distance from the bank.
It fell, to find the depths of that great sink.

'Astounding things,' I told myself, 'are bound      115
to come at this astounding sign, which now
my master follows with his waiting eye.'

How cautious we must always be when faced      118
with those who, far beyond observing deeds,
can gaze in wisdom on our very thoughts.

So now he said: 'There soon shall rise what I      121
expect (what you in thought now dream) will come.
All shall be, soon, uncovered to your eyes.'

Always, to every truth that looks, in face,      124
like lies, one ought (quite firmly) bar the lip
lest, guiltless, what one says should still bring shame.

I cannot, though, be silent here. Reader,      127
I swear by every rhyme this comedy
has caused to chime (may it not lack long favour)

that now, through dark and fatty air, I saw –      130
to strike sheer wonder in the steadiest heart –
approaching us a figure swimming up,

as any diver might who'd gone below      133
to loose an anchor snagged on rocks (or something
other, hidden in the sea) and now comes back,

arms stretching high, legs drawn to make the stroke.      136

# CANTO 17

<table>
<tr><td>1</td><td>'Behold! The beast who soars with needle tail<br>through mountains, shattering shields and city walls!<br>Behold! The beast that stinks out all the world!'</td></tr>
<tr><td>4*</td><td>To me, my lord spoke thus, then beckoned up<br>the monster to approach the jutting prow<br>that marked the end of all our marble paths.</td></tr>
<tr><td>7</td><td>It came, that filthy image of deceit.<br>Its head and trunk it grounded on the shore.<br>It did not draw its tailpiece to the bank.</td></tr>
<tr><td>10</td><td>The face was that of any honest man,<br>the outer skin all generosity.<br>Its timber, though, was serpent through and through:</td></tr>
<tr><td>13</td><td>two clawing grabs, and hairy to the armpits,<br>its back and breast and ribcage all tattooed<br>with knot designs and spinning little whorls.</td></tr>
<tr><td>16*</td><td>No Turk or Tartar wove a finer drape,<br>more many-coloured in its pile or tuft.<br>Nor did Arachne thread such tapestries.</td></tr>
<tr><td>19</td><td>Compare: on foreshores, sometimes, dinghies stand<br>in water partly, partly on the shingle –<br>as likewise, in the land of drunken Germans,</td></tr>
<tr><td>22</td><td>beavers will do, advancing their attack.<br>So did this beast – the worst that there can be –<br>there on the rocky rim that locks the sand.</td></tr>
<tr><td>25</td><td>Out into emptiness it swung its tail,<br>and twisted upwards its venomous fork.<br>The tip was armed like any scorpion's.</td></tr>
</table>

My leader said: 'We need to bend our path                    28
a little further down, towards that vile
monstrosity that's lolling underneath.'

So down we went, towards the right-hand pap.                  31
Ten paces, and we'd reached the very edge,
stepping well clear of flames and burning shoals.

And then, on getting to that spot, I saw,                     34
a little further on along the sandbar,
a group just sitting near the gaping waste.

And here my teacher said: 'To carry back                      37
experience of the ring that we're now in,
go over there and look at their behaviour.

But do not stay to talk at any length.                        40
Till you return, I'll parley with this thing,
for him to grant us use of his great thews.'

So once again, along the outward brow                         43
of Circle Seven I progressed alone
to where there sat these souls in misery.

The pain they felt erupted from their eyes.                   46
All up and down and round about, their hands
sought remedies for burning air and ground.

Dogs in the heat of summer do the same,                       49
stung by the bluebottle, gadfly and flea,
swatting at swarms with paw pads or with snout.

On some of these – these faces under showers                  52
of grievous, never-ceasing rain – I set my eyes.
I recognized no single one, but noticed

around the neck of each a cash bag hung                        55
(each with its own insignia and blaze),
on which their staring eyes appeared to graze.

So I, too, gazing, passed among them all,                     58*
and saw, imprinted on a yellow purse,
a blue device, in face and pose a lion.

Then, as my view went trundling further on,                   61
I saw another, with a blood-red field –
the goose it bore was whiter, far, than butter.

64       And then I heard (from one whose neat, white sack
was marked in azure with a pregnant sow):
'What are you after in this awful hole?

67       Do go away! Yet you – as Vitaliano is –
are still alive. Then understand me, please:
he'll sit on my left flank, my one-time neighbour.

70       I'm Paduan, among these Florentines,
and often they all thunder in my ears:
"Oh, let him come," they'll scream, "that sovereign knight,

73       who'll bring the bag that bears three rampant goats."'
At which, in throes, he wrenched his mouth awry
and ox-like curled his tongue to lick his nose.

76       And I, who feared that, if I lingered long,
I'd irritate the one who'd said 'Be brief',
now turned my back upon these worn-out souls.

79       My leader, I discovered there, had jumped
already on that fearsome creature's rump.
'Come on,' he urged, 'be stalwart and courageous.

82       From now on we'll descend by stairs like these.
Mount at the front so I can come between,
to see the tail won't bring you any harm.'

85       Like someone shivering as the grip of 'flu
spreads over him, pale to the fingernails,
who trembles merely at the sight of shade . . .

88       well, that was me, as these words carried over.
The threat of shame, however, when one's lord
is near, emboldens one to serve him well.

91       I settled down between those gruesome shoulders.
I wished to say (my voice, though, would not come):
'Yes. Please! Be sure you hold me very firm.'

94       He, who in many an earlier 'perhaps'
had aided me, as soon as I got on,
flinging his arms around me, hugged me tight,

97       and said: 'Go on, then, Geryon. Cast out!
Wheel wide about to make a smooth descent.
Think of the strange new burden on your back.'

Slowly astern, astern, as ferries leave          100
the quay where they had docked, so he moved out.
Then, only when he felt himself ride free,

he turned the tail where breast had been before,    103
and – stretching long, as eels might do – set sail,
paddling the air towards him with his paws.

No greater fear (so, truly, I believe)       106*
was felt as Phaeton let the reins go loose,
and scorched the sky as still it is today,

nor yet by ill-starred Icarus – his loins    109
unfeathering as the wax grew warm – to whom
his father screamed aloud: 'You're going wrong!'

And then with fear I saw, on every side,    112
that I was now in air, and every sight
extinguished, save my view of that great beast.

So swimming slowly, it goes on its way.    115
It wheels. It descends. This I don't notice –
except an upward breeze now fans my face.

By then I heard, beneath us to the right,    118
the roar of some appalling cataract.
And so I leant my head out, looking down.

More timorous of falling still, I saw    121
that there were fires down there and heard shrill screams.
Trembling, I huddled back and locked my thighs.

And then I saw, as I had not before,    124
the going-down – the spirals of great harm –
on every side now coming ever nearer.

A falcon, having long been on the wing,    127
and seeing neither lure nor bird to prey on,
compels the falconer to sigh: 'You're coming in,'

then sinks down wearily to where it left so fast.    130
A hundred turns – and then, far from its lord,
it lands, disdainful, spiteful in its scorn.

So, too, did Geryon, to place us on the floor,    133
the very foot of that sheer, towering cliff.
And then, unburdened of our persons now,

vanished at speed like barbed bolt from a bow.    136

# CANTO 18

<sup>1</sup>*    There is in Hell a place called Rottenpockets,
rock, all rock, its colour rusted iron,
as is the wall that circles all around.

4    Dead in the centre of that poisoned plain
a well yawns open – empty, broad and deep.
Of that (when it's 'convenient') I'll have my say.

7    For now, between the well mouth and the clench
of cliff, a circling belt goes round, its floor
divided into ten deep trenches.

10    Compare: to guard the outer walls of castles,
moats in concentric multiples are dug,
and form the figure of a wheel around them.

13    That was the pattern that these trenches made.
And where, from fortresses, pontoons run out
to link each threshold to the other shore,

16    so, at the bottom of the precipice,
radials ride over every bank and ditch
till, at the pit, they're stopped and then sucked in.

19    This was the place where – shaken from the spine
of Geryon – we found ourselves. The poet
took the left-hand fork. I followed in his track.

22    Then, to my right, I saw fresh suffering:
new whips, new torments and new torturers,
and Pocket One, with these, was all a-flutter.

25    Down in those depths, stark naked, there were sinners
who came, on this side of a line, face on,
and faster, in our direction, on the other.

The Romans, in the Jubilee, devised      28*
a way for pilgrims and pedestrians,
in all their multitudes, to cross the Bridge

so that, on one side (making for Saint Peter's),      31
they faced the Castle and, conversely, took
the other lane when heading for the Hill.

This way, that way, over the dismal rock,      34
there were (I saw them!) horny demons lashing,
lashing at the rear with vicious scourges.

Ouch! Even at the first stroke they lifted      37
their trotters; and none of them, for certain,
stayed for second helpings – fewer still for thirds.

But then, as I was moving on, looks clashed,      40
my own and one of theirs. I said straight off:
'There's one I've seen before. Once was enough.'

To get him in my sights, I stopped my stride;      43
and, pausing quietly along with me,
my guide now let me turn a short way back.

The body beaten abased its gaze, as if      46
it thought he really could hide. That didn't work.
'You there,' I said, 'Eyes-down! Bashful, are we?

Assuming that your profile's not a lie,      49*
then you are Venedico Caccianemico.
So what brings you to this killing pickle?'

And he to me: 'I grudge you my reply.      52
You and your bright words grind one out of me,
and make me call the world that was to mind.

Foul tittletattle got this right. It's me;      55
I fixed it. My sister Ghisolabella
did let the marquis have his way with her.

Don't think, though, I'm the only Bolognese      58
who's here in tears. The place is full of us.
Between the rivers Sàvena and Reno,

far fewer tongues speak "yes" as "yeah" than here.      61*
And if you want to get this straight, recall
what money means to Bolognese hearts.'

64      And, as he spoke, a devil now struck out:
'Push off, you pimp,' he said, and swung his lash.
'There aren't tarts here for you to turn to cash.'

67      I turned to join my escort once again,
and walked with him a few steps further on,
then reached an outcrop jutting from the bank.

70      We made our way quite easily up that,
then, turning right along the splintered ridge,
we left that bunch to endless circulation.

73      So now we came to where the vault gapes wide
to let those beaten beings pass beneath.
'Pause here,' said Virgil, 'and ensure some glimpse

76      of all these woebegones now marks your eye.
They go in our direction. So, as yet,
you've had no chance to look them in the face.

79      We saw from that decrepit bridge the traces
of a second crew. These came towards us.
These, as well, were driven by whistling whips.

82      I did not prompt him, but my mentor said:
'Look at that hero there, advancing now!
He seems, for all his pain, to shed no tear.

85*      How great an air of majesty he still retains!
He is that Jason who, astute and strong,
made Colchos grieve to lose its gold-fleeced ram.

88      Journeying on, he passed the isle of Lemnos,
where cold and reckless women had, by then,
delivered death to every living male.

91      Yet he, with hints and eloquence of phrase,
beguiled the young Hypsipyle – a girl
who had herself proved guileful to the rest.

94      Alone he left her there, alone, with child.
That crime incurs for him this penalty
which also stands as vengeance for Medea.

97      Along with him go all who turned such tricks.
And that's enough to know about this vale,
or else of those who're caught within its fangs.'

We'd come already to the point at which 100
the tight path crosses with the second bank
and makes a shoulder to another arch.

And now we heard, from Pocket Number Two, 103
the groans and griping of another lot,
the snuffling of their snouts, their slapping palms.

The banks were crusted with a slime and mould 106
that rose up in porridgy exhalations
and, scuffling, violated eye and nose.

The bottom of that pit goes down so deep 109
we saw it only when we climbed the ridge
and stood to see the rock rise straight above.

Reaching that point and looking down, we saw 112
that all of them were plunged in diarrhoea
flowing, it seemed, from human cubicles.

And while my eyes were searching deep within, 115
I noticed one whose head was foul with shit.
Had he the tonsure? It was hard to tell.

But he screamed out at me: 'Why gawp like that, 118
so hungry-eyed for me and not the other swill?'
'Because,' I said, 'if I remember well,

I've seen you once before, with drier coiffure. 121*
You are from Lucca. Alessio Interminei.
And that is why I've got my eye on you.'

He answered (battering his turnip top): 124
'I'm sunk this deep because of flatteries –
none were too sickly for my tongue to speak.'

When that was done, my leader now went on: 127
'Just poke your nose a little further out.
Your eyes may then be able to detect

a slut down there – filthy, with tangled hair, 130
scratting herself with cacky fingernails,
squatting at one time, upright at the next.

Thais! She's there, the whore, the one who cooed 133*
to her hot panting swain ("Yeees! Good for you?"),
"Angel, a miracle! My thanks indeed!"

Let that be all that here we need to view.' 136

# CANTO 19

1*     You! Magic Simon, and your sorry school!
Things that are God's own – things that, truly, are
the brides of goodness – lusting cruelly

4*     after gold and silver, you turn them all to whores.
The trumpet now (and rightly!) sounds for you.
There you all are, well set in Pocket Three.

7     Onwards towards this yawning tomb, mounting
the ridge, by now we'd reached its summit –
the point that plumbs the middle of the ditch.

10     O wisdom in the height, how great the art
that you display in Heaven, on earth and even
in that evil world! How justly you deal power!

13     I saw how all the livid rock was drilled
with holes – along its flanks, across its floor –
all circular, and all of equal measure.

16*     To me they seemed, in radius, no more nor less
than fonts that, in my own beloved Saint John's,
allow the priest at baptisms a place to stand.

19     (Not long ago, I shattered one of those.
Someone was drowning there. I got them out.
This, sealed and sworn, is nothing but the truth.)

22     Out of the mouth of every single hole
there floated up a pair of sinner feet,
legs to the ham on show, the rest concealed.

25     The soles of all these feet were set alight,
and each pair wriggled at the joint so hard
they'd easily have ripped a rope or lanyard.

As flames go flickering round some greasy thing 28
and hover just above its outer rind,
so these flames also, toe tip to heel end.

'Who, sir,' I said, 'is that one there? That one 31
who jerks in pain far greater than his *cònfreres*,
sucked at by flames more fiercely vermilion.'

'I'll lift you down,' he answered me, 'if you 34
insist. We'll take that bank the easier.
He'll talk to you himself about his twists.'

'Whatever pleases you,' I said, 'to me is good. 37
Lord, you remain: I'll not depart – you know –
from what you will. You read my silent thoughts.'

So on we went to the fourth embankment. 40
We turned around, descended on our left,
arriving at that pitted, straitened floor.

My teacher, kindly, did not set me down – 43
nor loose me from his hip hold – till we'd reached
that fissure where (all tears) shanks shuddered.

'Whatever you might be there, upside down, 46*
staked, you unhappy spirit, like a pole,
if you,' I said, 'are able, then speak out.'

So there I stood like any friar who shrives 49
the hired assassin – head down in the earth –
who calls him back to put off stifling death.

And he yelled out: 'Is that you standing there? 52*
Are you there, on your feet still, Boniface?
The writings lied to me by quite some years.

Are you so sick of owning things already? 55
Till now, you've hardly been afraid to cheat
our lovely woman, tearing her to shreds.'

Well, I just stood there (you will know just how) 58
simply not getting what I'd heard come out,
feeling a fool, uncertain what to say.

Then Virgil entered: 'Say this – and make speed: 61
"No, that's not me. I am not who you think."'
And so I answered as he'd said I should.

64     At which – all feet – the spirit thrashed about,
then, sighing loudly in a tearful voice:
'So what is it you want of me?' he said.

67     'If you're so keen to know who I might be,
and ran all down that slope to find me out,
you'd better know I wore the papal cope.

70     A true Orsini, son of Ursa Bear,
I showed such greed in favouring her brats
that – up there well in pocket – I'm in pocket here.

73     Below me, in great stacks beneath my head,
packed tight in every cranny of the rock,
are all my antecedents in the Simon line.

76     Down there I'll sink, in that same way, when he
arrives whom I supposed that you might be,
and uttered, therefore, my abrupt inquiry.

79     But I already – feet up on the grill, tossed
upside down – have passed more time
than Boniface yet will, stuck here with red hot toes.

82*     For after him from westwards there'll appear
that lawless shepherd, uglier in deed,
who then, for both of us, will form a lid.

85     He shall be known as a "Jason-Once-Again".
We read in Maccabees: "Priest Bribes a King."
This other will score well with one French prince.'

88     I may have been plain mad. I do not know.
But now, in measured verse, I sang these words:
'Tell me, I pray: what riches did Our Lord

91     demand, as first instalment, from Saint Peter
before He placed the keys in his command?
He asked (be sure) no more than: "Come behind me."

94     Nor did Saint Peter, or the rest of them,
receive from Matthias a gold or silver piece,
allotting him the place that Judas lost.

97*     So you stay put. You merit punishment.
But keep your eye on that ill-gotten coin
that made you bold with Charles the Angevin.

And, were I not forbidden, as I am,           100
by reverence for those keys, supreme and holy,
that you hung on to in the happy life,

I now would bring still weightier words to bear.    103
You and your greed bring misery to the world,
trampling the good and raising up the wicked.

Saint John took heed of shepherds such as you.    106*
He saw revealed that She-above-the-Waves,
whoring it up with Rulers of the earth,

she who in truth was born with seven heads    109
and fed herself, in truth, from ten pure horns,
as long as she in virtue pleased her man.

Silver and gold you have made your god. And what's    112
the odds – you and some idol-worshipper?
He prays to one, you to a gilded hundred.

What harm you mothered, Emperor Constantine!    115*
Not your conversion but the dowry he –
that first rich Papa – thus obtained from you!'

And all the time I chanted out these notes,    118
he, in his wrath or bitten by remorse,
flapped, with great force, the flat of both his feet.

My leader, I believe, was very pleased.    121
In listening to these sounding words of truth,
he stood there satisfied, his lips compressed.

So, too, he took me up in his embrace.    124
Then, bodily, he clasped me to his breast
and climbed again the path where he'd come down.

Nor did he tire of holding me so tight.    127
He bore me to the summit of that arch
spanning the banks of Pockets Four and Five.

And there he gently put his burden down,    130
gently on rocks so craggy and so steep
they might have seemed to goats too hard to cross.

From there, another valley was disclosed.    133

# CANTO 20

1   I now must turn a strange new pain to verse
    and give some substance to this twentieth chant
    that deals (*Cantica* 1) with sunken souls.

4       Already I had set myself to peer
    intently on those now-discovered depths,
    washed as they were with agonizing tears.

7       I saw there people circling round that trench.
    And on they came in silence, weeping still –
    as slow in pace as litanies on earth.

10      Then, as my gaze sank lower down these forms,
    each was revealed (the wonder of it all!)
    twisted around between the chin and thorax.

13      The face of each looked down towards its coccyx.
    And each, deprived of vision to the front,
    came, as it must, reversed along its way.

16      Seized by some paralytic fit, others,
    perhaps, have been so turned awry. But I –
    not having seen, myself – don't credit it.

19      That God may grant you, as you read, the fruit
    that you deserve in reading, think, yourselves:
    could I have kept my own face dry, to see,

22*     close by, that image of our human self
    so wrenched from true that teardrops from the eyes
    ran down to rinse them where the buttocks cleave?

25*     Of this, be sure: that, leaning on a spur
    of that unyielding cliff, I wept. 'Are you,'
    my escort said, 'like them, an idiot still?

    Here pity lives where pity's truth is dead.        28
Who is more impious, more scarred with sin
than one who pleads compassion at God's throne?

    Lift up your head! Stand straight. See, that one there?    31*
Under his chariot wheels, the earth yawned wide;
and Thebes – all eyes – yelled: "Where, Amphiaraus,

    headlong away? Why leave us in this strife?"    34
Into the ceaseless void he fell, until
he came where Minos stands, who seizes all.

    He's formed his chest – amazingly – from shoulder.    37
As once he wished to see too far ahead,
his tread is backward, and he stares to rear.

    See there Tiresias! Male-to-female switch.    40*
His looks, mutating, were entirely changed,
his members altering till each was each.

    And then, to win once more his virile plumes,    43
he needs must strike a second time, and shake
again at coupling snakes his witch's wand.

    Then, spine to gut, the prophet Arruns comes.    46
High in the Lunigiana hills – over
Carrara homesteads, so hard-hoed by serfs –

    he found a grotto in the marble cliffs    49
and took this for his dwelling place. Nothing,
from there, cuts off the view of sea or star.

    And then there's one whose breasts you cannot see    52*
(since these are mantled by her flowing strands)
who shows on that side all her shaggy fleece.

    She, once, was Manto, scouring many lands,    55
until she reached and settled at my birthplace.
And so – to please me – listen for a while.

    Her father, having left this life – and Thebes,    58
the place of Bacchus, being now in thrall –
for years she travelled, searching through this world.

    Above, in lovely Italy, there lies a lake    61*
(in Latin: Benacus) beneath those Alps
that lock out Germany beyond the high Tyrol.

64      From waters gathered in that standing pool
a thousand springs, I think, or more, refresh
the lands between those peaks, Camonica and Garda.

67      There is a place, the central point of these,
where pastors – if they choose to sail from Brescia,
from Verona and from Trent – have power to bless.

70      Here that brave citadel Peschiera sits,
built where the shoreline sinks to reach a low,
boldly outfacing Bergamese and Brescians.

73      Cascading from the lap of Benacus,
waters, unstayably, must run down here.
Through lush green meadows these all form a stream.

76      And this, when it begins to run, is known
by name as Mincio, not Benacus.
(It meets the river Po around Govérnolo.)

79      Moving, the Mincio at once dips down,
then, broadening in the plain, it forms a marsh –
and this in summer can be foul and brackish.

82      Manto, that bitter virgin, passing by,
saw, in the centre of that great morass,
a place unploughed and bare of population.

85      There, fleeing still from human fellowship,
she settled with her vassals, plied her arts,
in this place lived, here left her empty corpse.

88      Then other peoples came who had, so long,
been scattered all about. Because the marsh
surrounded it, the site was safe and strong.

91      They raised their city over those dead bones.
They called it Mantua (no magic charm!),
since Manto first had made the place her own.

94      Those living there were once more numerous,
before the idiotic Casalodi was
so taken in by Pinamonte's trick.

97      So, if in other stories you should hear
some tale of how my city came to be,
don't let the truth, I urge, be mocked by lies.'

'Sir,' I replied, 'to me your words are sure,                    100
and capture so entirely what I think,
that differing versions are as burned-out coal.

But let me know some more of this parade,         103
that is, if any here still merit note.
My mind is waiting only for that word.'

And so he said: 'The one who there fans wide      106*
his beard from cheek to shadowed shoulderblade,
was – in those years when Greece was void of men,

when, even in the cradle, boys were few –         109
an augur. He, with Calchas, cast the hour
at which to cut the anchor rope in Aulis.

By name Eurypylus, there is some verse            112
in my great tragedy that sings of him.
But you'll know where. You know the whole thing through.

And then we meet, so withered in his flanks,      115*
a certain Scotsman, Michael. In the spheres
of fraud and magic, he was full of pranks.

There's Guido Bonatti. Look! Asdente, too!        118*
The cobbler must be wishing now he'd stuck
to thread and leathers. Too late to repent.

Then see those hags? They, one and all, forsook   121
for witchcraft distaff, needle, pin and spool.
They cast their spells with weeds and ju-ju dolls.

But come, now come. The zone where hemispheres    124*
both meet by now is gripped (and, under
Seville, waves are touched) by Cain, his bush and thorns.

And yestere'en the rounding moon was full.        127
You must remember this. It shone while you,
unharmed, were deep within that first dark wood.'

And so he chatted on and we fared forwards.       130

# CANTO 21

1      So on we went from bridge to bridge, speaking
of things that I shan't, in my comedy,
commit to song. We gained the brow. Once there,

4      we paused and, down in Rottenpockets, saw
another fissure still, more empty tears.
I saw it all – a marvel of mere dark.

7*      Compare: Venetians in their Arsenal,
in winter when their ships cannot set sail,
brew up a viscous pitch which they then smear

10      on ailing boards, or else lay down new hulls.
Others will plug the ribs of hulks that have,
by now, made many a long-haul trip.

13      Some hammer at the prow, some at the poop,
some whittle oars, where others plait the rig.
Some mend the mainsail, others patch the jib.

16      So here – though more by art of God than fire –
a dense black gunge was brought to boiling point,
and splashed on all the banks in sticky smears.

19      I saw this stuff but nothing else within
but bubbles as the boiling bubbled on,
swelling to roundness, glue-ily sinking in.

22      In mesmerized amazement I just gazed.
But then, 'Look out! Look out!' my leader cried,
then dragged me, where I'd stood, towards his side.

25      And there I turned as one who may well pause –
all swagger, in his sudden panic, gone –
to peep at what he really ought to flee,

yet, glimpsing this, does not delay his parting.                    28
I saw there, right behind us, this black demon
running the ridge around in our direction.

Eek! How ferocious all his features looked.                         31
How viciously his every move seemed etched,
wings wide apart, so lithe and light of foot.

The hunch blades of his shoulders, keen and proud,    34
bore up the haunches of some criminal,
his hook fixed firm in tendons at each heel.

Mounting our bridge, demonically he barked:              37*
'Get this, Rotklors! A boss man from Lucca!
You lot can dunk him. I'll get back for more.

I've got it stuffed, Saint Zita's place, with this sort.    40
They're at it there, the lot. (Oh! Not Bonturo!)
Cash on the nail, and "no" becomes "for sure".'

Dumping his load, he then dashed down                        43
and crossed the flinty slope. No mad bullmastiff
ever was loosed so fast to catch a thief.

The sinner dived, but then turned, writhing up.          46
At which the demons, dossing by that bridge,
yelled: 'No place, black face, here for black-faced gods.

You can't swim here like bathers in the Serchio.        49
If you don't want to know what hooks can do,
then just don't poke your nose above that tar.'

They sank in him a hundred barbs or more.                 52
'Down here,' they sang, 'you'll tango in the dark!
Get under cover! Pull what scams you can!'

Chefs do the same. They get their kitchen boys          55
to fork the centre of a simmering pot,
so chunks of meat do not float up too high.

Here, too. 'Seem not to be here,' Sir now said.           58
'Just hunker down behind a spur of rock.
It may still offer you some place to hide.

Yet have no fear. Oppose me as they may,                   61
my strategy – I know what's what – is clear.
I've been involved in rucks like this before.'

64      So now, beyond the bridge head, on he went,
and needed, when he neared Embankment Six,
the steadiest front that he could summon up.

67      With all the fury and tempestuous rage
of dog packs rushing on some poor old tramp –
who freezes there and pleads from where he'd reached –

70      so now those demons underneath the arch
stormed out at him and brandished all their hooks.
But he cried out: 'Don't even think of it.

73      Before you set on me with curving prongs,
let one of you who'll hear me out draw near,
and then discuss if hooking me is right or wrong.'

76      So, 'Go on, Rottentail,' they shrieked. 'That's you!'
And he advanced (the others kept their ground
and muttered: 'What will he get out of it?')

79      'Do you imagine, Rottentail,' my teacher said,
'who've seen me come already once, immune
to all your tricks, that I am here without

82      the favouring aid of fate or will divine?
Let us pass on. For Heaven wills that I
should guide another on the savage way.'

85      His arrogance at this took such a fall
he let his hook slip, dangling, to his heels.
'OK,' he told the others, 'let's not cut him.'

88      And now my leader turned and said: 'O thou
who sittest there, squatting by that splintered bridge,
return to me with confidence renewed.'

91      So shift I did, and reached him speedily.
At which the demons all came pressing forwards –
so I could not be sure they'd keep their word.

94*     In this way, at Caprona once I saw
the infantry come edging out, despite
safe conduct, chary of the hordes around.

97      Huddled against my leader's side, pressed hard
along him, head to toe, I could not wrench
my eyes from them. Their looks did not look good.

They cocked their barbs. Then one spoke out:    100
'Want me to touch him on his fat backside?'
And they replied: 'Yeah, get him in the notch.'

But then that devil who was still in speech    103
with my great leader swung around at speed,
and said: 'Just cool it, cool it, Tangletop!'

'Further along this crag,' he now declared,    106
'you just can't go. Bridge Six is broken down.
It lies in ruins on the valley floor.

But if you'd care to schlepp still further on,    109
then do so round this arching cliff. Nearby,
another outcrop makes a path for you.

Just yesterday (five hours ahead of now),    112*
a thousand years, two centuries and sixty-six
from when the path was cut had then elapsed.

I'll send in that direction some of mine,    115
to watch for any sinner scenting air.
You go with them. They won't dare pull a stunt.'

'So, forward, Crackice! Forward, Flash Ali!'    118*
so he began: 'And Baddog! You as well.
And you, old Twirlitufts, can lead the squad.

Loveslot as well. And you, too, Dragonrunt,    121
Bigpig with tusks, and also Skratcherker,
Flutterby! For'ard! And you there, mad Glogob!

Search all around this pan of boiling lime:    124
until you reach the spur that arcs, unbroken,
over these dens, these two will go unharmed.'

'Sir, sir,' I said, 'what's this I see! Please, sir,    127
if you know how and where, let's go alone.
Myself, I didn't ask for this at all.

Your eyes are usually so very keen.    130
Can you not see? Just look! They grind their teeth.
Their frowns are warnings of what harm they mean.'

His answer was: 'I wouldn't have you frightened.    133
Let them scowl so, and grind as they may choose.
They mean it for the souls in this sad stew.'

136      About-face, leftwards on the rocky pass,
each poked a tongue, teeth clenched, towards their lord,
and he – to give the order now, 'Quick march!' –
139      in answer made a trumpet of his arse.

# CANTO 22

I, in my time, have seen brave knights strike camp,          1
parade their power, launch an attack, and then,
at times, to save their skins, desert the field.

Yes, you, Aretines, I have seen our cavalry          4*
charge through your heartland. Skirmishes I've seen,
cut-and-thrust tournaments and running duels,

all to the sound of horns (at times) or bells,          7*
to beating drums or signals flashed from ramparts,
devices of our own and more exotic signs.

Yet never to so weird a pipe or whistle          10
have I, till now, seen foot or horse fall in,
nor ship set sail to signs like that, from land or star.

So, on we went, five friends on either side.          13
What fearsome company! Well, that's the way it is:
hobnob in church with saints, in pubs with sots.

The tar pit called for all my concentration          16
to note each facet of this rotten hole,
and also of the persons burning there.

As schools of dolphin when they arch their spines          19
provide a signal to the mariner,
to say the ship should soon be steered back home,

so too from time to time, to ease their pain,          22
a sinner gave his back some air, then quick
as any lightning flash would hide again.

Likewise, in ditches at the water's edge,          25
bullfrogs will stand, their snouts alone on show,
their feet concealed, with all their bulk below.

28    In this same way, these sinners lolled around.
      But then, whenever Twirlitufts came past,
      they swiftly dived beneath the bubbling crust.

31    I saw – at this, my heart still skips a beat –
      that one (as happens when a frog school springs,
      but one stays dallying) was left behind.

34    And Skratcherker – as being nearest to him –
      enmeshed his hook among those tar-caked locks
      and yanked him out like any floppy otter.

37    I knew them all by name, the lot of them.
      I'd noted each when they were first enrolled,
      and then, between them, heard them call out names.

40    'Get in there, Glogob! Get him with your hook!'
      (So, in damned unison, the chorus shrieked.)
      'And tear the leather off his ugly rump!'

43*   I turned, and to my master said: 'Find out,
      if you can manage it: who is that so-and-so
      who's fallen foul of these antagonists?'

46    My leader went, and stood beside him there,
      wanting to know the place where he was born.
      He answered: 'I'm a native of Navarre.

49    My mother, having borne me to a lout,
      who brought himself and all he had to ruin,
      engaged me to the service of a nobleman.

52    And then I joined King Thibaut's retinue,
      to practise arts of chartered bribery.
      For which I pay my dues in this great heat.'

55    Then Bigpig, with his boar-like jowls – a tusk
      stuck out from both his cheeks – supplied a sip
      of how well one of these could rake and rip.

58    The mouse had got among the bad cats now.
      But Twirlitufts enclosed him in his arms.
      'Stay over there!' he said. 'I'll keep him pinned.'

61    He tilted up his face towards my guide:
      'Go on, then. Ask him, if you want still more.
      But quick,' he said, 'before they do him in.'

'So tell me, then,' my master now went on,                       64
'among the criminals beneath the tar,
are any – can you tell? – Italian?' 'Just now,'
    he answered me, 'I left a man from there.          67
If only I were with him still beneath the lid,
I wouldn't need to dread these hooks and claws.'

    'We've taken quite enough of this!' So said        70
the Loveslot. Skewering an arm, he sliced
a muscle out in one long hookful.

    Then Dragonrunt must also have a go.                73
He ogled the ham. But their decurion
swung round and gave them all a filthy frown.

    Then, just a little, they all settled down.        76
The sinner lay there, wondering at his wound.
My lord without delay now turned and asked:
    'Who was the one from whom, you say, you took,     79*
ill-fatedly, your leave to reach this shore?'
'Brother – as was – Gomita!' he replied.

    'Sard from Gallura, vessel of deceit!              82
Palming (well-greased) his sire's worst enemies,
he treated all so well, each sang his praise.

    He took their cash, then let them off the hook.    85
In this – as he'll admit – and everything
a total crook. Not small time, though. The King!

    Don Michael Zanche, from the Logudor,              88
still hangs around with him. Their tongues don't tire
of banging on about "Sardin-i-ah".

    Ow! Look at how that demon grinds his teeth.        91
I could tell more but (oh! I'm terrified!)
he means to come and give my scabs a scrub!'

    The high commander swung on Flutterby,              94
whose moon eyes popped in eagerness to pounce.
'Butt out!' he hissed. 'You vulture! Over there!'

    Witless with fear, he started once again:           97
'If you would witness or hold audience
with Lombards or Tuscans, I can make them come.

100      But let these Rotklors all stand well aside –
and no one need be frightened they'll attack –
while I, just sitting on this self-same spot,

103      will whistle. Now I'm here alone. Presto!
And now we're seven! That's our usual trick
when any from below gets out of it.'

106      Hearing this blag, old Baddog twitched his snout,
then shook his head and snarled: 'The little demon!
He means to take a dive and get back in.'

109      That sinner up his sleeve had snares galore.
'O yeah! That's me,' he said. 'A demon! Sure!
Really? You think I'd bring my gang more grief?'

112      Flash Ali, at these words, could not hold back.
Despite what his companions thought, 'Go on,'
he said. 'Slope off. I'll not come galloping.

115      I will, though, stretch my wings across the pitch.
Let's leave the ridge. Let's make the slope our screen.
And then we'll see if you can get off clean.'

118*      O you there, as you read! Get this! Olympics!
They all then turned to face the other bank,
even the one who first was most reluctant.

121      The Navarrese chose his moment well.
Feet firmly planted, in a single flash,
he'd leapt and gone, scot-free of their intent.

124      At this, the lot of them were pierced by guilt.
Yet, undeterred, the devil most at fault
drove onwards. 'Now you're for it!' he yelled out.

127      To no avail. No wing could overhaul
the speed of fear. The sinner plunged. Square on,
the demon baulked and then shot up again.

130      So, too, a rapid duck dives down, glimpsing
a falcon closing in. The duck's foe then
returns aloft, bitter in thwarted pique.

133      Crackice, still seething at the doublecross,
zoomed ever onwards in his yen to see
the sinner free – then mix it with Flash Ali.

So, since the barrator had long since gone,      136
he turned his talons on his own best mate.
Above the ditch he locked him in his prongs.

The other, though, a right old sparrowhawk,      139
returned the hook. And so the two of them,
as one, went tumbling to the boiling pond.

The heat that instant made them come unhitched.      142
But, even so, they couldn't raise a thing,
so tightly glued together were their wings.

Then Twirlitufts, condoling with his kin,      145
sent four of them towards the inner rim,
with all their grappling tackle, at top speed.

This side and that they went to take their posts,      148
and bent their hooks towards those two, stuck fast.
By now they both were crisped within the batter.

With that entanglement, we left the matter.      151

# CANTO 23

|    |                                                            |
|----|------------------------------------------------------------|
| 1  | Silent, alone with no one now beside us,                   |
|    | we went our way – the one behind, the other                |
|    | leading on – walking as meek Franciscans do.               |
| 4* | My mind turned (thinking of that scuffle still)            |
|    | to Aesop and his fables, most of all                       |
|    | the one about the frog and rat and hawk.                   |
| 7* | For 'now' and 'noo' are hardly more alike                  |
|    | than this fine mess to that – if parallels                 |
|    | are rightly drawn between the start and finish.            |
| 10 | But thoughts pop up and then lead on to more.              |
|    | So from this first a further set was born,                 |
|    | which now redoubled all my earlier fears.                  |
| 13 | 'Because of us,' the sequence ran, 'that lot               |
|    | have been so injured, put on, tricked and scorned,         |
|    | they cannot fail, I think, to be upset.                    |
| 16 | Suppose their bile gets tangled now with anger,            |
|    | then surely they'll come after us and snarl                |
|    | more viciously than dogs that snout a hare.'               |
| 19 | I felt already that my every curl                          |
|    | was bristling, on its end. So, gazing back,                |
|    | stock still, I said: 'If you, sir, do not hide             |
| 22 | yourself this second, me as well . . . I dread             |
|    | the Rotklors gang. They're not now far behind.             |
|    | I hear them now, imagine it, quite clear.'                 |
| 25 | 'If I,' he said, 'were leaded mirror glass,                |
|    | I could not make your outer image mine                     |
|    | more swiftly than I grasp your inward stress.              |

Your thoughts just now came in upon my own,                     28
in bearing similar, and look as well.
These, all together, formed a single plan.

　　Suppose that, on the right, the incline's such               31
that we can reach the pocket there beyond,
we shall elude the hunt we now imagine.'

　　No sooner had he offered up this thought                     34
than, coming after us, I saw them, wings
stretched wide, now closer, meaning to get us.

　　My leader in an instant caught me up.                        37
A mother, likewise, wakened by some noise,
who sees the flames – and sees them burning closer –

　　will snatch her son and flee and will not pause,            40
caring less keenly for herself than him,
to pull her shift or undershirt around her.

　　Down from the collar of that circling rock,                 43
backwards he launched himself, and met the slope
that forms a bung against the other trench.

　　No mill race ever ran through any sluice                     46
at such velocity, or streamed to meet
the scoops that drive, on land, the grinding stone,

　　as now my master slithered down that verge,                 49
bearing me with him, bound upon his breast,
as though I were his son and no mere friend.

　　And hardly had his feet touched down to meet                52
the pocket floor than those were at the summit,
over us. We need have had no worries.

　　For that exalted providence that chose                       55
such ministers to guard Ditch Five also
deprived them of the power to ever leave.

　　We found, down there, a people painted bright.              58
Their tread, as round they went, was very slow,
weeping, worn down and seemingly defeated.

　　They all wore robes with hoods hung low, that hid           61*
their eyes, tailored – in cut – to match those worn
by monks who thrive in Benedictine Cluny.

64\*     So gilded outwardly, they dazed the eye.
        Within, these robes were all of lead – so heavy
        those capes that melt in torture would have seemed mere str

67      What labour to eternity to wear such dress!
        We took once more the leftward path along
        with them, intent on their distress and tears.

70      Because, though, of the labouring weight they bore,
        these weary folk came on so slow that we,
        at every hip swing, joined new company.

73      'Do all you can' – I put this to my guide –
        'to find here someone known by name or deed.
        As we move onward, scan around to see.'

76      Then one who'd recognized my Tuscan words
        from close behind yelled out: 'You! Racing there
        through all this murky air, just ease your stride.

79      You'll get, perhaps, from me what you desire.'
        At this my leader turned. And, 'Wait,' he said,
        'then follow forwards at the pace he sets.'

82      I stopped and saw there two who, from their look,
        (though hampered by their load and narrow footings)
        in mind were speeding on to reach my side.

85      At last, they caught me up. With eyes a-squint,
        they gazed at me in wonder, spoke no word,
        till muttering they turned and, each to each:

88      'This one, it seems – Just see his throat! It flicks! –
        is still alive. If dead, why favoured so,
        to go uncovered by a weighty cloak?'

91      And then to me direct they said: 'Tuscan,
        you've reached the college of the hypocrites.
        Do not disdain to say who you might be.'

94      'Born,' I replied, 'by the lovely Arno,
        grown in the city that adorns its banks,
        I still am in the limbs I've always worn.

97      But who are you, in whom, as I can see,
        great pain distils such tears upon your cheeks?
        What punishment strikes out these sparks from you?'

And one replied to me: 'These orange robes          100
are thick with such a quantity of lead,
the weight of them would make a balance creak.

We're good-time friars, Bolognese both.          103*
Our names? I'm Catalano. Loderingo's there,
captured together in that town of yours –

although, by custom, there is one alone          106
whose mandate is to keep the peace. Our doings
still appear around the Watch, for such we were.'

I then began: 'O brothers! All the harm that you . . .'          109
but said no more. Straight to my sight, there sped
one crucified. Three staves fixed him to earth.

And he, on seeing me, writhed all around          112
and fluffed his beard up with the sighs he heaved.
Then brother Catalan, who saw all this,

revealed to me: 'This figure, staked, whom you          115*
so wonder at, advised the Pharisees
that one man suffer for the sake of all.

Across the road, stretched naked, as you see,          118
he first must feel, whoever passes by,
the toiling weight of those who come this way.

Here too lies Annas – father of his wife –          121
racked in this ditch with others of that house
that proved an evil seed bed for the Jews.'

Virgil, I saw, just stood there marvelling,          124
bending above that figure on the cross,
eternally in ignominious exile.

But then, towards the friar he voiced: 'Please say          127
(though not to trouble you), if you're allowed,
is there some outlet lying to the right

through which the two of us can make our way          130
without the need to call black angels here,
who might come down to further our departure?'

'Far sooner than you hope,' the answer was,          133
'we'll near a rock that, jutting from the Ring,
vaults over all these savage valley floors –

136      except it's broken here and forms no covering.
You can, though, clamber up the ruined side.
The slope is gentle and the base piled high.'

139      My leader stood a moment, head hung down.
And then he said: 'He gave a false account,
that hooker-up of sinners over there.'

142      'I, in Bologna,' so the friar said, 'have heard
a good few stories told of devil vice,
not least "Old Nick's a liar – falsehood's dad".'

145      At this, with lengthened pace, my lord strode off,
clear signs of anger flitting on his face.
And so I left these beings with their loads

148      to follow in the prints of his dear feet.

# CANTO 24

In that still baby-boyish time of year,                    1*
when sunlight chills its curls beneath Aquarius,
when nights grow shorter equalling the day,

  and hoar frost writes fair copies on the ground          4
to mimic in design its snowy sister
(its pen, though, not chill-tempered to endure),

  the peasant in this season, when supplies                7
run short, rolls from his bed, looks out and sees
the fields are glistening white, so slaps his thigh,

  goes in, then grumbles up and down, as though            10
(poor sod) he couldn't find a thing to do,
till, out once more, he fills his wicker trug,

  with hope, at least. No time at all! The features        13
of the world transform. He grabs his goad.
Outdoors, he prods his lambs to open pasture.

  In some such way, I too was first dismayed               16
to see distress so written on my leader's brow.
But he, as quickly, plastered up the hurt.

  And so, arriving at the ruined bridge,                   19
my leader turned that sour-sweet look on me
that first he'd shown me at the mountain foot.

  He spread his arms, then, having in his thought          22
surveyed the landslip, and (a man of sense)
assessed it well, he took me in his grip.

  Then, always with adjustments in his moves               25
(so that, it seemed, he foresaw everything),
in hauling me towards the pinnacle

28      of one moraine, he'd see a spur beyond
and say: 'Next, take your hold on that niche there.
But test it first to see how well it bears.'

31      This was no route for someone warmly dressed.
Even for us – he, weightless, shoving me –
we hardly could progress from ledge to ledge.

34      Had not the gradient been less severe
than that which faced it on the other side,
I'd have been beat. I cannot speak for him.

37      But Rottenpockets slopes towards the flap
that opens on the lowest sump of all,
and so, in contour, every ditch is shaped

40      with one rim proud, the other dipping down.
So, in the end, we came upon the point
where one last building block had sheared away.

43      My lungs by now had so been milked of breath
that, come so far, I couldn't make it further.
I flopped, in fact, when we arrived, just there.

46      'Now you must needs,' my teacher said, 'shake off
your wonted indolence. No fame is won
beneath the quilt or sunk in feather cushions.

49*     Whoever, fameless, wastes his life away,
leaves of himself no greater mark on earth
than smoke in air or froth upon the wave.

52      So upwards! On! And vanquish laboured breath!
In any battle mind-power will prevail,
unless the weight of body loads it down.

55*     There's yet a longer ladder you must scale.
You can't just turn and leave all these behind.
You understand? Well, make my words avail.'

58      So up I got, pretending to more puff
than, really, I could feel I'd got within.
'Let's go,' I answered, 'I'm all strength and dash.'

61      Upwards we made our way, along the cliff –
poor, narrow-going where the rocks jut out,
far steeper than the slope had been before.

Talking (to seem less feeble) on I went,                                    64
when, issuing from the ditch beyond, there came
a voice – though one unfit for human words.

I made no sense of it. But now I neared                                     67
the arch that forms a span across that pocket.
The speaker seemed much moved by raging ire.

Downwards I bent. But in such dark as that,                                 70
no eye alive could penetrate the depths.
But, 'Sir,' I said, 'make for the other edge,

and let us then descend the pocket wall.                                    73
From here I hear but do not understand.
So, too, I see, yet focus not at all.'

'I offer you,' he said to me, 'no answer                                    76
save "just do it". Noble demands, by right,
deserve the consequence of silent deeds.'

So where the bridgehead meets Embankment Eight                              79
we then went down, pursuing our descent,
so all that pocket was displayed to me.

And there I came to see a dreadful brood                                    82
of writhing reptiles of such diverse kinds
the memory drains the very blood from me.

Let Libya boast – for all her sand – no more!                               85
Engender as she may chelydri, pharae,
chenchres and amphisbaenae, jaculi,

never – and, yes, add Ethiopia, too,                                        88
with all, beyond the Red Sea, dry and waste –
has she displayed so many vicious pests.

And through all this abundance, bitter and grim,                            91*
in panic naked humans ran – no holes
to hide in here or heliotropic charms.

Behind their backs, the sinners' hands were bound                           94
by snakes. These sent both tail and neck between
the butts, then formed up front the ends in knots.

And near our point, at one of them (just look!)                             97
a serpent headlong hurled itself and pierced
exactly at the knit of spine and nape.

100      Then, faster than you scribble 'i' or 'o',
         that shape caught fire, flash-flared and then (needs must)
         descended in cascading showers of ash.

103      There, lying in destruction on the ground,
         the dead dust gathered of its own accord,
         becoming instantly the self it was.

106*     Compare: the phoenix (as the sages say)
         will come to its five-hundredth year, then die,
         but then, on its own pyre, be born anew.

109      Its lifelong food is neither grass nor grain,
         but nurture drawn from weeping balm and incense.
         Its shroud, at last, is fume of nard and myrrh.

112      The sinner, first, drops down as someone might
         when grappled down, not knowing how, by demons
         (or else some other epileptic turn),

115      who then, on rising, gazes all around,
         bewildered by the overwhelming ill
         that came just now upon him, sighing, staring.

118      So, too, this sinner, getting to his feet.
         What power and might in God! How harsh it is!
         How great the torrent of its vengeful blows!

121*     My leader then demanded who he was.
         'I pelted down' – the sinner, in reply –
         'to this wild gorge, right now, from Tuscany.

124      Beast living suited me, not human life,
         the mule that once I was. I'm Johnny Fucci,
         animal. Pistoia is my proper hole.'

127      I to my leader: 'Tell him, "Don't rush off!"
         and make him say what guilt has thrust him down.
         I've seen him. He's a man of blood and wrath.'

130      The sinner, hearing this, made no pretence.
         He fixed on me a concentrated eye,
         and coloured up in brash embarrassment.

133      'It pisses me right off,' he then declared,
         'far more than being ripped away from life,
         that you have got to see me in this misery.

I can't say "no" to what you ask of me.       136
I'm stuck down here so deep 'cos it was me,
the thief who nicked the silver from the sanctuary.

    Then I just lied – to grass up someone else.       139
You won't, however, laugh at seeing this.
If ever you return from these dark dives,

    prick up your ears and hear my prophecy:       142*
Pistoia first will slim and lose its Blacks.
Then Florence, too, renews its laws and ranks.

    Mars draws up fireballs from the Val di Magra,       145
wrapped all around in clouds and turbulence.
And these, in acrid, ever-driven storms,

    will battle high above the Picene acre.       148
A rapid bolt will rend the clouds apart,
and every single White be seared by wounds.

    I tell you this. I want it all to hurt.'       151

# CANTO 25

1*    His words now reached their end. And then the robber
hoisted hands on high – a fig-fuck formed in each –
and screamed: 'Take that! I'm aiming, God, at you!'

4    From that point on, the serpents were my friends.
For one entwined its length around his neck
as if to say: 'I'd have him speak no more.'

7    And then another bound his arms down tight,
and clinched itself so firmly round the front
he could not shake or shiver in either limb.

10*    Pistoia! Ah! Pistoia! Why not take a stand?
Just burn yourself to blackened ash, and be
no more. Your seed succeeds in doing only ill.

13*    In all of Hell, through every murky ring,
I saw no spirit facing God so proud,
even that king flung down from Theban walls.

16    Away he fled. He spake no further word.
And then there came, I saw, a wrathful centaur.
'Where? Where is he,' he called, 'so sour and crude?'

19    Maremma, I should think – with all its swamps –
has fewer snakes than he. They writhed from rump
to where, on human features, lips begin.

22    Above its shoulders, stretched behind the nape,
there lay a dragon, wings extended wide.
And all it hits against, it sets on fire.

25*    'This centaur,' so my teacher said, 'is Cacus.
He is the one – so many times – who caused
a lake of gore to flood the Aventine.

He does not tread the path his brethren take.    28
For spying, once, a mighty herd at hand,
he made it all his own by furtive fraud.

    Beneath the mace of Hercules (that god    31
rained down a hundred blows, and he, perhaps,
felt ten, no more) his devious doings ceased.'

    So Virgil spoke. The centaur sped away.    34
But now three spirits had approached beneath,
though neither of us noticed they were there

    until they shouted out: 'So who are you?'    37
Our story-telling pausing at this point,
we fixed attention wholly on that trio.

    Among the three was none I recognized.    40
And yet it chanced – as happens many times –
that one was forced to speak another's name,

    inquiring: 'Where has Cianfa got to now?'    43*
At which (to shut my leader up) I placed
a finger slantwise from my chin to nose.

    If you are slow, my reader, to receive,    46
in faith, what I'll say now – no miracle.
I saw it all, and yet can scarce believe.

    While, eyebrows raised, I stared at these three men,    49
a reptile hurled itself with all six feet
at one, front on, and took a total hold.

    It clenched the belly with its middle claws.    52
With each anterior it seized an arm.
It sank a forked fang deep in either cheek.

    Along each loin it slithered out a leg,    55
then struck its tail between the two, to take,
now upwardly, a grip around the buttocks.

    Ivy in tangles never barbed to tree    58
so tight as this ferocious awfulness,
linking its limbs in tendrils round that trunk.

    As though the two were formed of warming wax,    61
each clung to each and, mingling in their hues,
neither now, seemingly, was what it was.

64   Like that, a flame runs flaring up a page
     and, just ahead, goes ever-darkening tints,
     not black as yet, and yet the white still dies.

67   The other two, at this, stared on. And each
     moaned out: 'Ohimé, Agnello, how you change!
     Already, look, you're neither two nor one.'

70   And yes, those two by now were both as one.
     That is: the outlines of the two appeared
     in one face only, two-ness lost and gone.

73   Two arms were fashioned out of four long strips.
     Thorax and stomach, loins and thighs and hips
     became such organs as you've never seen.

76   In each, the primal signs were all struck out.
     Two yet not either, as it seemed, this sick
     apparition. So, treading slow, it went its way.

79   The great green lizard, at the summer's height,
     lashed by a dog star rage from hedge to hedge,
     crosses the path as though a lightning flash.

82   So, paunch high (darting at the two, of three,
     who still remained), inflamed and fierce, there came
     a snakelet, livid as a peppercorn.

85   This serpent pierced in one that spot where first
     we draw our nourishment, transfixing him.
     It then fell back, stretched out before his face.

88   The one transfixed gazed down but spoke no word.
     Rather, he yawned, his feet just planted there.
     Sick sleep, it seemed, had struck him hard, or fever.

91   He eyed the snake. The reptile eyed him back.
     Each gave out smoke in streams – the wound of one,
     the serpent's jaws. The smoke streams slowly met.

94*  Lucan! Be silent now, and tell no more
     your snaky tales of poor Sabellus and Nasidius.
     Give ear to what the bow will now unleash.

97   Ovid, be silent! Less 'Cadmus' and 'Arethusa'!
     In turning verse, these two he may convert
     to snake or stream. I do not envy him.

For he, through metamorphosis, did not  100
compose two species, glance on glance, whose forms
disposed themselves exchanging actual substance.

Each answered each in working through this rule:  103
the serpent fashioned (from his tail) a fork;
the wounded human dragged his footprints to.

The legs, now fastening at their inner thighs,  106
adhered so well that soon the join between
gave no clear sign of ever having been.

The cloven tail assumed the figure now  109
of that which, over there, was lost to view.
Hide softened here, but hardened over there.

I saw each arm retract and reach its pit.  112
The paws, conversely, of that stubby newt
lengthened as much as human feet grew short.

The hindmost toes then curled around and clinched;  115
these formed the member that a man conceals.
The other wretch wrenched his own part in two.

As now, around this pair, the fumes still hang,  118
a gauze of stranger colours – causing hair
to sprout fresh here, while there it plucks it sleek –

the one rose up, the other fell down flat,  121
yet, peering out, as this snout changed for that,
neither could wrest from either evil eye beams.

Upright, the one dragged jowl across to temple.  124
And then, from leakages of surplus pulp,
a pair of ears appeared, on thinned-out jowls.

Whatever residue did not run back  127
now gelled, and gave that face its human nose.
The lips, plumped up to meet the need, gained bulk.

The other, lying flat, extends his muzzle.  130
Then, just like snails when pulling in their horns,
he draws his ears back, flush along his skull.

And now the tongue – once whole, and quick to speak –  133
divides in two. The other finds his fork
has closed right up. The furls of smoke now cease.

136*  The soul, transmogrified to fearful beast,
  flees – hissing, snuffling – off across the pit.
  Spot on his track, the speaking presence spits.

139  And then he turns on him his novel back
  to tell the third: 'I'll see slick Buoso go
  as I did, bellyflop, around this track.'

142  Zymotic in the seventh bilge, I saw, then,
  change and counterchange. My only plea, if here
  my pen turns vain, must be sheer novelty.

145  And though my vision was a bit confused
  (spirit quite drained of all its energies),
  these souls could not so covertly pass by

148*  that I should fail to see the cripple Puccio.
  Of three companions who had first come there,
  he, all alone, escaped from alteration.

151  The last was him that you, Gaville, weep for.

# CANTO 26

Rejoice, Florentia! You've grown so grand          1*
that over land and sea you spread your beating wings,
and through the whole of Hell your name resounds.

Among those thieves and robbers there, I found,          4
were five of your own citizens. I am ashamed.
And you do not acquire, by this, great honour.

Yet if we dream, near dawn, of what is true,          7*
then you, not long from now, will surely feel
what Prato aches to see for you – others, as well.

And were it now it would not be too soon.          10
Would it were so, as rightly it should be.
It weighs me down the more that time drags on.

We now moved off. And climbing by those stairs          13
that, going down, had bleached us ivory,
my leader, mounting up, pulled me along.

And so, proceeding on this lonely way          16
through splintered rocks and outcrops from the ridge,
feet without hands would not have gained advantage.

It grieved me then, it grieves me now once more,          19
to fix my thoughts on what I witnessed there.
Now, more than usual, I must hold mind back,

lest brain should speed where virtue does not guide.          22
Thus if, by some propitious star (or more),
I've come to good, I'd best not make it void.

A farmer, leaning on his hillside, rests.          25
(It's summer time, when he who lights the earth
least hides his face from us.) This countryman,

28       as now the fly makes way for the mosquito,
         sees there, below him on the valley floor,
         (where he perhaps will plough and gather grapes)

31       glow-worms in numbers such as now I saw,
         glittering around the dip of Pocket Eight,
         when I arrived there, looking to its depths.

34*      Compare, as also in the Book of Kings:
         Elisha (once avenged by furious bears)
         beheld Elijah's chariot drawn away

37       by horses rising to the Heavens, straight.
         His eye, unable to pursue, could see
         only the flame, like cloud whisp, rising high.

40       So, too, within the gullet of that ditch,
         these fires move round. None shows its thievery.
         Yet each fire stole some sinning soul away.

43       I stood there on the bridge and craned to look.
         Indeed, had I not clutched a nearby rock,
         I surely would (unpushed) have fallen in.

46*      My leader, who had seen how hard I gazed,
         informed me now: 'In all these fires are souls.
         Each one is swaddled in its inward blaze.'

49       'Well, sir,' I answered, 'to be told by you,
         I am, of course, the surer. Myself, though,
         I'd already thought of that. I meant to ask:

52*      "Who comes within that cloven-crested flame
         that seems to rise as from that pyre where, once,
         Eteocles was laid beside a brother slain?"'

55       'Within this flame,' so he now said, 'suffering,
         are Ulysses and Diomed. As one, they face
         their nemesis, as they in rage were one.

58       Within their flame, the crime is now bewailed
         of those whose cunning wrought the Trojan horse –
         the door that freed the noble seed of Rome.

61       They mourn as well the ruse by which – though dead –
         young Deidamia must weep Achilles' loss.
         They're punished, too, for theft, of sacred statues.'

'If they, within those tongues of fire, can speak,                     64
I beg you, sir,' I said, 'and beg again –
so may each prayer be worth a thousand more –

that you do not forbid my waiting here                                 67
until that flame with horns has come this way.
You see I bend to it with great desire.'

'Your prayer,' he said, 'is worthy of great praise,                    70
and I, most willingly, accede to it.
But you must keep your tongue in tight control.

Leave me to speak. For I know very well                                73*
what you desire. Nor would these two be quick,
perhaps, to hear your words. They both are Greek.'

And when the flame had reached, in time and place,                     76
a point at which my leader thought it fit,
I heard him form his utterances thus:

'O you there, two within a single flame,                               79
if I, when living, won, in your eyes, merit,
if merit, whether great or small, I won –

in penning my exalted lines of verse –                                 82
do not move on. Let one of you declare,
where, lost, he went, to come upon his death.'

The greater of those horns of ancient flame                            85*
began to tear and waver, murmuring
as fires will do when struggling in a wind.

Drawing its pinnacle this way and that,                                88
as though this truly were a tongue that spoke,
it flung its utterance out, declaring: 'Once

I'd set my course from Circe (she had kept                             91*
me near Gaeta for a year or more,
before Aeneas, passing, named it that),

no tenderness for son, no duty owed                                    94
to ageing fatherhood, no love that should
have brought my wife Penelope delight,

could overcome in me my long desire,                                   97
burning to understand how this world works,
and know of human vices, worth and valour.

100*      Out, then, across the open depths, I put to sea,
a single prow, and with me all my friends –
the little crew that had not yet abandoned me.

103      I saw both shorelines (one ran on to Spain,
the other to Morocco), Sardinia
and all those islands that our ocean bathes.

106      I and my company were old and slow.
And yet, arriving at that narrow sound
where Hercules had once set up his mark –

109      to warn that men should never pass beyond –
I left Seville behind me on the right.
To port already I had left Ceuta.

112      "Brothers," I said, "a hundred thousand
perils you have passed and reached the Occident.
For us, so little time remains to keep

115      the vigil of our living sense. Do not
deny your will to win experience,
behind the sun, of worlds where no man dwells.

118      Hold clear in thought your seed and origin.
You were not made to live as mindless brutes,
but go in search of virtue and true knowledge."

121      My men – attending to this little speech –
I made so keen to take the onward way
that even I could hardly have restrained them.

124      Wheeling our stern against the morning sun,
we made our oars our wings in crazy flight,
then on, and always leftward making gain.

127      Now every star around the alien pole
I saw by night. Our own star sank so low
it never rose above the ocean floor.

130      Five times the light that shines beneath the moon
had flared anew – and five times, too, grown dim –
since we had set our course on that high venture.

133      Ahead of us, a mountain now appeared,
darkened through distance, soaring (to my eyes)
higher by far than any ever seen.

We cheered for joy. This quickly turned to tears.   136
For now a wind was born from that new land.
Twisting, it struck at our forward timbers.

The waves and keel three times it swirled around.   139
And then a fourth. The afterdeck rose up,
the prow went down, as pleased Another's will,

until once more the sea closed over us.'   142

# CANTO 27

1      The flame was upright now, and still. It meant
to say no more. And so (the poet gently
gave his leave) it went its way, away from us.

4      But close behind, another blaze came up,
and made us turn (a sound, confusedly,
had issued out) and glance towards its top.

7*     Compare the Torture bull of Sicily.
This bellowed its inaugural – and justly so –
with wailings from the smith who'd filed it smooth –

10     these bellows echoing its victim's moans –
so that, although, in form mere hollow bronze,
it was, it seemed, transfixed with living pains.

13     So now those words which, dreadfully, could find
no vent or outlet from their burning source,
were spoken in an accent of their own.

16     But when these sounds had made their way along,
and reached the tip which gave that flick and twist
that tongues will give to any stream of air,

19*    we heard: 'You there! I square my words at you.
I heard you say – in Lombard tones – just now:
"Be out of it! I'll rile on you no more."

22     I'm here, perhaps belatedly. But you,
I hope, will not be loath to stay and speak.
You see how far from loath I am. And I burn!

25     If you have fallen even now to this
blind world, leaving the land of lovely Italy
(from which I carried any guilt I share),

tell me: Romagna – is it peace or war?                    28*
I was myself from those Urbino hills,
the mountain yoke that first unlocks the Tiber.'

I held my head bowed low attentively,                     31
until my leader lightly touched my side,
saying: 'You speak. This one's from Italy.'

And I, who had indeed got words prepared,                 34
began without delay to speak to him:
'You, then, below! The soul that's hidden there!

Your dear Romagna (despots all the lot)                   37
is not without, nor ever was, some war-at-heart.
On leaving, though, I saw no open conflict.

Ravenna stands as she has stood for years.                40
The Eagle, blazon of the Clan Polenta,
broods in her skies; its vanes hide even Cervia.

Forlì (her towers withstood that lengthy siege            43
that left a blood-stained pile of French invaders)
goes ever on beneath the green-clawed Lion.

The Mastiffs, old and young, of Fort Verucchio,           46
vicious in lordship over Lord Montagna,
still, as is usual, gnash and suck their bone.

And where Lamone and Santerno flow,                       49
the towns are schooled by Lion's-Whelp-sur-Argent.
Summer to winter, north to south, he cants.

And then that place whose rim the Savio bathes –          52
between the mountain and the plain it lies;
it lives between high tyranny and freedom.

So, who are you? I beg you now to say.                    55
If you still wish your name to brave the world,
be no more stiff than others are with you.'

The flame, as was its wont, first roared a while.         58
Then, to and fro it writhed its pointed peak
and finally pronounced this speaking breath:

'Should I suppose, in answering, I spoke                  61
to any person who should ever see
the world again, this flame would shake no more.

64     But since, if all I hear is true, there's none
who ever yet, alive, escaped these deeps,
I may reply without the fear of infamy.

67     I, once great warlord, was a friar next,
believing, bound by cord, I'd make amends.
And my beliefs would all have been assured,

70     had not there been (he'll rot!) that sovereign priest
who won me, firmly, back to former sins.
*Qua re* and "how" I mean that you should hear.

73     While I was still, in form, such pulp and bone
as, first, my mother gave to me, actions
of mine all favoured rather fox than lion.

76     Stratagems, wiles and covert operations –
I knew them all. These arts I so pursued
that word of me rang out throughout the world.

79     But when I recognized that now I'd come
to where we all in life ought, properly,
to furl our sail and take our rigging in,

82     whatever once had pleased me now annoyed.
I vowed – repentant, shriven – all obedience.
It might (what misery!) have worked out well.

85*     The foremost lord of our new Pharisees,
who waged in Rome a war around the Lateran
(never, of course, with Jew or Saracen;

88     his foes were faithful Christians everyone;
none had been present at the fall of Acre,
none worked as trader in the Sultan's souks),

91     did not, considering his own account,
consult his office or his holy rule,
nor mine – that cord which makes its wearer thin.

94     As once, on Mount Soracte, Constantine
required that Pope Silvester cure his leprosy,
so he, mi-lording it, commanded me

97     to cure him of his fevered arrogance.
He asked advice, and I maintained my silence.
He seemed plain drunk in what he had to say.

But still he urged: "Don't let your heart be doubtful.   100
I grant you henceforth total absolution.
Teach me how Penestrina may be razed.

The power is mine (you know it well) to unlock   103
Heaven's door. Or lock it fast. Hence these two keys.
My predecessor held them far from dear."

Such points – all weighty – drove me to the view   106
that silence now was worse than quick assent.
"Father," I answered, "since you wash away

the sin that I must now be guilty of,   109
some promise – generous though of mean extent –
assures you triumph from your lofty throne."

Now dead, Saint Francis came for me. But then   112*
a black alumnus of the Cherubim
cried out: "Don't cheat! *You* can't dispose of him.

Down must he come, to join my squalid thralls.   115
His sound advice was, after all, deceitful.
And since that hour, I've hovered round his hair.

Repentance fails? There can't be absolution,   118
nor penitence when willing ill goes on.
That is, by contradiction, *impossibile*."

The pain I felt! I shook myself awake.   121
To me he said (he took a grip): "Perhaps
you never knew: I practise logic, too."

To Minos he transported me, who then –   124
eight times! – coiled tail around relentless spine.
In utter ire, he bit this thing, and then

declared: "Condemned is he to thievish fire."   127
So that is why, as you see here, I'm lost,
and thus go dressed in inward bitterness.'

And once it reached the end of these few words,   130
grieving, the flame went off along its way,
thrashing its horn and wrenching it awry.

We now – my lord and I – went further on,   133
rounding the ridge to find another arch
to span Ditch Nine – wherein, a fee is paid,

incurred by those who force fair deals apart.   136

# CANTO 28

1*     Who could relate – even in words set loose
from rhyme, even by telling it over and over –
all that I witnessed now, the blood, the wounds.

4     There is no doubt: all human speech would fail.
Our powers, whether of mind or tongue, cannot
embrace that measure of understanding.

7     Suppose that, gathered in one single whole,
were all those people of the fated South
whose blood was shed in pain on the Apulian fields –

10     be it as victims of the sons of Troy,
or else, as Livy writes unerringly,
in that long war where rings were heaped as spoils.

13     Then add all those who suffered grievous wounds
in wars against the Norman king, Guiscardo,
and also add that band whose bones are gleaned

16     at Ceperano still (where southerners, each one,
proved traitorous). To Tagliacozzo, then, move on.
There, ageing Elard won – by guile, not arms.

19     Were every lopped-off limb or part pierced through
seen once again, that, even so, would far
from equal all the foul display in Pocket Nine.

22     One I saw riven from his chin to fart hole.
No barrel – midslat or moon rib missing –
ever, I am certain, gaped as wide as that.

25     Between his legs his guts all dangled down,
innards and heart on show, and that grim bag
that turns to shit whatever gullets swallow.

My eyes were fixed and gazed on him alone.    28
And he gazed back. Then, opening up his thorax,
hands at work: 'Look now,' he said, 'how wide I spread!

You see how mangled is the great Mohammed.    31*
Ali, ahead, wends weeping on his way,
cloven in countenance from quiff to chin.

So, too, the others that you here observe,    34
all in their lives sowed schism, scandal, discord.
And that is why they all are here so splintered.

Back there a devil deftly decks us out    37
in these cruel ornaments, and crops each page
in every quire that comes upon his sword edge.

For, as we pass around this road of pain,    40
each wound and gash is made entire and whole
before we come to face him once again.

But who are you, who there sniff down at us    43
and so perhaps are slow to meet the harm
that you've been sentenced to for your own crime?'

'Death has not reached him yet,' my teacher said,    46
'nor is he drawn by guilt to any pain.
I, being dead, to give him full experience,

am bound to lead him all through Hell, from gyre    49
to gyre from ring to ring through every round.
And this, I tell you, is the simple truth.'

To hear this said, a hundred (or yet more)    52
stopped short. They looked in wonder from the ditch
at me, in awe, forgetting their own agony.

'Since you, perhaps, will shortly hail the sun,    55*
then say: If Fra Dolcino is not keen
to join me soon, he'd better stockpile well,

lest winter snow in drifts makes barriers    58
bestowing triumph on the Novarese,
which they'd not lightly come by otherwise.'

That was Mohammed who – as now to leave –    61
had raised his foot while uttering these words.
He placed it flat to ground and went his way.

64    Another then – his throat pierced through, his nose
shorn off and level with his hanging brows,
one ear alone, and only that to hear –

67    now paused with all the rest to stare at me,
but opened up, before the others might,
his windpipe, crimson in its outward parts.

70    'You there,' he said, 'whom guilt does not condemn,
I've met you once on our Italian soil,
unless I'm much beguiled by close resemblance.

73*    If you should see once more the lovely plain
that slopes between Vercelli and Marcabo,
then call to mind again Da Medicina.

76*    And let the two best men of Fano know
(Guido and Angiolello, his peer),
supposing that our foresight is not vain,

79    they'll both be slung, their necks bedecked with stones,
from boats that coast around Cattolica,
betrayed in this by a villainous baron.

82    From Cyprus on to the Majorcan isles,
Neptune has never seen a crime so great
pulled off by pirates or Argolian Greeks.

85    That traitor with his single seeing eye
(who rules a city that another with me here
might wish his sight had still to hunger for)

88    will work it so that they will come to parley,
then work it so they'll need no prayer or vow
to save them from the gales around Focara.'

91    And I in answer: 'Show me. Make it clear –
if you so wish I'll take back news of you –
who is that despot with the bitter view?'

94*    At which, he put his hand around the jaw
of one beside him, prising wide his mouth,
and yelled out: 'Here he is. And he can't utter.

97    Exiled, he drowned all Caesar's hesitations.
For, "Anyone," he said, "who's well prepared
will always suffer harm from titubation."'

How dismal and confused he seemed to be,                   100
his tongue hacked out and hollow in his gullet,
so headstrong once, this Curio, in parley.

Then one came round with both his hands cut off.           103
He raised his flesh stumps through the blackened air;
he made his face drip filthy red with blood,

and yelled: 'Me too! I'm Mosca, you'll recall,             106*
who said, alas: "What's done, well, that is done."
And this sowed evil seed for every Tuscan.'

To which I added: 'Death to all your clan!'                109
So, piling always grief on top of grief,
he went his way, a melancholic madman.

But I stayed there and, staring at the throng,            112
I now saw something which, without more proof,
I fear that I could never hope to speak of.

Conscience, though, lends me confidence to try.           115
That good companion renders all men free
under its breastplate, knowing we are pure.

I saw – I'm sure – and still I seem to now,               118
in company with others in that herd,
a torso striding by without a head,

who held that head, though severed, by the hair.          121
It swung as might a lantern from his hand.
'Alas!' it said, and stared at us in wonder.

Himself he made a lamp for his own light.                 124
So here were two in one and one in two.
How that can be He knows who orders so.

He stood directly by the bridge foot now.                 127
He raised an arm (so, therefore, head and all)
to throw his words the closer to us there.

And these words came: 'See this, the harm, the hurt.      130
Breathing you go still, watching on the dead.
See now: is any punishment as great?

And so you may return with news of me,                    133*
then know that I'm that Bertran de Born
who gave false comfort to the youthful king.

136\*      Father and son, I set at mortal odds.
No worse, with Absalom, Ahithophel,
whose evil promptings prodded David on.

139      Since persons so close-linked I put apart,
so I, alas, apart now bear my brain,
thus severed from its root in this great trunk.

142      In me, then, counter-suffering can be seen.'

# CANTO 29

This multitude, their wounds so various,                    1
had made my eyes (the lights I look by) drunk.
So now they wished to stand there, and just gaze.

But Virgil said: 'Are you still staring on?               4
Why is your seeing plunged so deep among
such miserable, mutilated shades?

You've not done this in any other pocket.                 7
Do you imagine you can count them all?
Well, think! This trench goes twenty miles around.

The moon already is below our feet.                       10*
The time that we're allowed to stay is short.
And much is yet to see that still you've not.'

'If you had only cared,' I answered him,                  13
'to know the reasons for that lingering look,
you would perhaps have let me stay still longer.'

But he (my leader), and myself behind,                    16
was pressing on. I answered thus,
and added, as I went: 'Within that den

where I just now, with reason, fixed my eye,              19*
there is a spirit of my blood who weeps,
grieving the guilt that, down there, sets its price.'

My teacher then: 'Allow no wave of thought                22
henceforth to break around his memory.
Attend to other things. And let him be.

I saw him standing by the bridge foot there,             25
still gesturing – a threatening finger raised –
and heard his name called out: Geri del Bello.

28      You were so caught, intent upon the sight
of that one there, once sire of Altafort,
you did not care to look around. So off he went.'

31      'His violent death,' I now addressed my lord,
'which goes yet unavenged by any kin,
whose fate must be to share this lasting shame,

34      inspires disdain in him. I judge that this
is why he left, speaking no word to me.
This all the more makes clear to me my duty.'

37      Our talk went on in such-like terms until
we found the jutting spur that showed (or would,
had there been light to see) the floor beyond.

40      I stood there high above the final cloister
of Rottenpockets. All its postulants
were present and revealed for us to see.

43      A host of lamentations shot around me,
their iron barbs sharp-tipped with pain and pity.
I covered up my ears with both my hands.

46*     Such sicknesses as here there'd be if all
contagions born of summer heat – from wards
throughout Sardinia, the Chiana Vale, Maremma –

49      were brought together in one single hole.
That's what it was, the stench that came from it,
a fetor rising as from rotting limbs.

52      Veering still leftwards as we always did,
we searched that ridge and reached its final crag.
And there more vividly I came to view

55      the depths in which, unerringly, the power
of justice – minister of One on High –
will castigate those known on earth as frauds.

58*     No greater woe, as I imagine it,
was ever, even in Aegina, known – where plague
infected every citizen and air

61      so dripped malignancy, its creatures all –
down to the smallest worm – fell, sickening fast.
This ancient race was then restored (so say

those poets who believe it true) by seed 64
of ants. Such woe appeared across the dark pit floor.
See, in their different stooks, the spirits languishing.

Some sprawled across the stomach of the next, 67
some over shoulders. Others, on all fours,
dragged on (to make a change) along the road.

Without a word, we went on, step by step, 70
still gazing at and listening to the sick.
They could not lift their bodies from the ground.

I saw there leaning, one against the next – 73
propped up as pairs of saucepans are to lose
their heat – two, scabby-spotted head to toe.

And never have I seen a currycomb 76
whisked (by a groom whose boss is waiting by,
or else disgruntled to be woken up)

so brisk as these attacked that raging itch – 79
for which no salve can ever now be found –
with biting fingernails to scrape at each.

With fingernails, each tore off showers of scabs, 82
as might a fish knife when it's skinning bream,
or else, perhaps, some type with larger scales.

'You there, whose fingers tear your chainmail off' – 85
to one of them my leader spoke these words –
'employing them as pincers sometimes, too,

now tell us (may your manicure endure, 88
your nails work well to all eternity!),
are there Italians sunk with you down there?'

'We, wrecked and ruined, are Italians both.' 91
So, weeping, one of them made this reply.
'But who are you that put to us this question?'

'I'm one,' my leader answered, 'who descends 94
with this still-living man from ledge to ledge.
My purpose is to show him all of Hell.'

At this, the coupling that had held them sheared, 97
and, trembling, each one turned himself to me,
as others did who heard these words in echoes.

100 My good, kind teacher came up close to me,
saying: 'Just tell him what it is you want.'
And so, as he now wanted, I began:

103 'So may the thought of you be never robbed
from human memories in the first of lives,
but live on brightly under many suns,

106 tell me who you might be, and of what kin.
Dread not – for all your foul and loathsome pain –
but openly make known yourselves to me.'

109* 'I was,' one answered, 'an Aretine once.
Albero of Siena had me burned alive.
But I'm not brought for what I died for here.

112 O yes! It's true, in jest I said to him:
"I've got the knowhow. I can fly through air."
Then he – all eyes, excited, but no genius –

115 was eager that I put my art on show.
I did not do a Daedalus. For that alone,
he got the one who called him son to burn me.

118 But Minos – not allowed to judge amiss –
condemned me to this final slot because,
in life, I practised as an alchemist.'

121 'On land or sea,' I turned towards the poet,
'was anyone as gormless as these Sienese?
Even the French aren't that idiotic.'

124* At which, the other leper, overhearing,
quipped in return: 'Except, of course, for Stricca,
who really knew what temperate spending is!

127 And Nick as well, the twit. He, in that garden
where the clove seed grows, discovered first
how rich the virtues of carnation are.

130 Omit, as well, those merry men with whom
Kid d'Ascian consumed both farms and vines.
Dazzledeye, too – who taught the boy such wisdom.

133 To see, however, who (like you) speaks here
so anti-Sienese, just sharpen up your eye.
My face – look hard – may give you your reply.

I am, you'll see, the shadow of Capocchio.     136
Alchemically, I falsified base metals
and, if I eye you well, then you'll recall
    how marvellous an ape of nature *I* was.'     139

# CANTO 30

1*     Think of that age when Juno – wracked with wrath,
so envious of Semele – expressed her spite,
over and over, against the blood of Thebes.

4     That was the time when Athamas ran mad.
He saw his wife who carried, as she went,
in either arm the load of their two sons,

7     and yelled: 'Come on! Let's spread those nets! I mean
to stalk them all, both whelps and lioness.'
He then stretched out his unrelenting claws.

10     He grasped one child (Learchus was his name).
He whirled him round. He dashed him on a stone.
His wife drowned, loaded with their second son.

13     When, likewise, ever-turning Fate brought down,
in flames, the Trojans from all-daring height –
and so, together, king and kingdom broke –

16     Hecuba, grieving, wretched, now enslaved,
first saw Polyxena, her daughter, dead,
and then – to find there, lain along the margin

19     of the sea, her youngest, Polydorus –
barked in her lunacy like any cur,
the pain of it so wrenched her mind askew.

22     And yet no fury known in Troy or Thebes
was ever seen, in anyone, to strike
so viciously at beast or human limb

25     as now I saw in two blank, naked shades –
who, racing round that circle, gnashed and gored
as swine do when their pigsty is unbarred.

One got Capocchio. At the very knot                        28
of neck and spine, his tusks sank in. Then round
the hard pit floor he hauled him, belly scraping.

The Aretine (still there) spoke all atremble:              31*
'That banshee idiot is Gianni Schicchi.
He rages on, and treats us all like that.'

'Really?' I answered. 'Well, let's hope his fangs          34
don't pierce your rear. But (not to trouble you),
please say who's that, before it springs away.'

'That soul is known in legend,' he declared.               37
'It's Myrrha the Depraved, beyond the bounds
of love (as love should be) her father's friend.

She made her way to meet him in that sin,                  40
shaping herself in counterfeit disguise.
So, too, the other, shooting off. To win

a mare (the queen of all the herd) he shaped               43
in counterfeit the guise of dying Buoso,
whose testament, attested thus, was sound.'

And now, when these two raging shades, on whom             46
till now I'd fixed my eye, had gone their way,
I turned and looked at other ill-created souls.

And one I saw was fashioned like a lute,                   49
or would have been if severed at the groin,
to amputate those parts where humans fork.

Dropsy (osmosis of a morbid flux):                         52
that discomposes, as the swellings rise,
all natural fit – so face and paunch mismatch –

constrained him, so his mouth hung open wide.              55
So, too, in fever victims, wracked with thirst,
one lip curls back, the lower meets the chin.

'O you who pass and know no pain (though why               58
I cannot understand) through this mean world,'
so he began, 'behold and hold in mind

the miseries of mastercraftsman Adam.                      61
I had, alive, my share of all I sought;
and now I crave, alas, the merest water drop.

64    Those brooks that trickle down the high green hills
      to reach the Arno from the Casentine
      and, as they run, make channels, chill and moist,

67        stand always in my sight. And not in vain:
      the image of them parches me far more
      than this disease that strips my face of meat.

70        Unbending justice probes me to the core.
      It takes its hint from regions where I sinned,
      meaning the more to put my sighs to flight.

73*       Here Fort Romena stands, and here I forged
      fake specie, printed with the Baptist marque.
      On that account, I left, up there, my body burned.

76        Yet could I only glimpse those woeful souls –
      Guido or Sandro or their brother – here,
      I'd not exchange the Branda Spring for that.

79        Already in, there's one of them, if those
      crazed shadows as they whirl around speak truth.
      What use is that to me? My limbs are bound.

82        If only I were still so light and lithe
      to travel in a hundred years one inch,
      already I'd have started on that path,

85        seeking him out from all this filthy clan.
      And this ditch turns eleven miles around.
      Nor is it less than half a mile across!

88        I'm only in this mess because of them.
      They led me on. I counterfeited florins
      so each contained three carats-worth of dross.'

91        'And who,' I said, 'are those two so-and-sos,
      steaming as wet hands do on winter days,
      those lying tight against your left frontier?'

94        'I found them here,' he said, '(they've not turned since)
      as soon as I showered down upon this midden.
      I do not think they'll budge in all eternity.

97*       Joseph was falsely charged by that "she" there.
      The other, just as false, is Sinon (Trojan-Greek!).
      Their biting fever brews that curdled reek.'

Then one of them, who took it much amiss – 100
or so I'd guess, to hear his name so sullied –
now thumped that tight-stretched belly with his fist.

It rumbled forth as though it were a drum. 103
Adam (the master) countered with his arm
to strike him no less hard across the face,

and said: 'It may well be I cannot move, 106
seeing how heavy I've become in limb.
But still my arms are free to do the job.'

The answer came: 'You weren't as free as that 109
when, arms trussed up, you went to mount the pyre.
Your arms were free, though, in their forging days.'

'There,' the hydroptic said, 'you speak mere truth. 112
Yet, as a witness, you were not so true
at Troy, when true words were required of you.'

'Well, I spoke false, and you struck dodgy coin. 115
But I'm here,' Sinon said, 'for one plain fault.
You were accused of more than any demon.'

'The horse! Remember that, you lying cheat!' 118
(This came in answer out of Swollenguts.)
'Tough luck on you that all the world knows that.'

'And tough on you,' the Greek replied, 'the thirst 121
that cracks your bloated tongue, the bilge that swells
that belly to a hedgerow round your eyes.'

At which: 'Yeah, yeah' (the coiner). 'Sickness 124
has stretched your mouth (what's new?) to tearing point.
I may be dry. I'm swollen, ripe with pus.

But you're burnt-out. Your sick head throbs and aches. 127*
It wouldn't take too much – a word or so –
to make you lick the mirror of Narcissus.'

All ears, I strained to listen in – until 130
I heard my teacher speak: 'Go on! Just gaze!
It won't take much for me to fight with you.'

And when I heard his words, so near to wrath, 133
I turned towards him with a shame that still,
on calling it to mind, brews vertigo.

136    Like someone dreaming of a harm to come,
who, dreaming, yearns for this to be some dream,
and hence desires what is as though it weren't,

139    so was I now. For wishing I could speak,
and so excuse myself, I so excused myself,
and did not think that all along I did.

142    'Less shame,' my master said to me, 'makes clean
far greater fault than yours has been. And so
cast off the weight of all your misery.

145    Consider well. I'm always by your side.
Remember this, if Fortune leads you on
to where such spats as this are played out loud.

148    To wish to hear such stuff is pretty low.'

# CANTO 31

The self-same tongue that bit me first so hard                    1
that both my cheeks had coloured up, bright red,
now offered once again its remedy.

So, too (as I have heard the story told),                         4*
the spear that both Achilles and his father bore
would cause a wound that spear alone could cure.

We turned our back upon the dismal deep,                          7
riding the bank that circles it around,
and made our way across without more speech.

Here it was less than night and less than day,                    10
so that our seeing went no way ahead.
But then I heard a horn ring out so loud

that thunder in comparison is vapid,                              13
and, turning back to see the echoing source,
I fixed my eyes upon one single place.

After the great and grievous rout at which                        16*
was lost the sacred band of Charlemagne,
great Roland sounded notes of no such terror.

I had not held my head turned there for long                      19
when (so it seemed) I now saw many towers.
And therefore, 'Sir,' I said, 'what town is this?'

'Because,' he said, 'through all these wreaths of shade           22
you rush ahead too far from what's at hand,
you form of it a blurred and empty image.

You'll see quite clearly when you soon arrive                     25
how greatly distance may deceive the sense.
So drive yourself a little further on.'

28       Then, with great tenderness, he took my hand.
He then went on: 'And yet before we step
ahead – so all these facts may seem less odd –

31       you ought to know that these aren't towers.
         They're giants.
These stand within the well around its rim,
navel height downwards, all the lot of them.'

34       As when a mist is thinning out, the gaze
will, point by point, begin to recompose
the figure hidden by the steam-thick air,

37       so, boring through that dense, dark atmosphere,
approaching ever closer to the edge,
false knowledge fled and fear grew yet more great.

40*      For, as above its circling curtain wall,
Montereggione boasts a crown of towers,
so too above the bank that rings the well

43       stood, towering here to half their body height,
the dreadful giants, who are under threat
from highest Jove whenever he wields thunder.

46       By now I saw, in each of these, the face,
the chest and shoulders, areas of paunch,
and, down the ribcage, all their dangling arms.

49       Nature did well, desisting from the art
of forming animals like that. She thus
deprived great Mars of his executors.

52       If she, on that account, did not repent
of whales and elephants, to subtle minds
this will seem right, and most intelligent.

55       For when the powers of working intellect
are wed to strength and absolute illwill,
then humans cannot find a place to hide.

58*      In bulk and length, his face could be compared
to that bronze pine cone in Saint Peter's, Rome.
His other bones were all in due proportion.

61*      And so that bank (his fig leaf, 'zone' or apron,
hanging around his loins below) displayed,
above, up to his mane, as much of him

as three tall Frisians would boast in vain.      64
I saw their thirty-eight-inch finger spans
down from the point where cloaks are buckled on.

   '*Raphèl maì amècche zabì almì,*'      67
so screaming it began, that fearsome mouth,
unfit to utter any sweeter psalm.

   My leader aimed: 'You idiotic soul!      70
Stick to your horn. With that, give vent to wrath,
or any passion that you chance to feel.

   Just fumble round your neck, you great dumb thing.      73
You'll find the cord it's tied to. There it rests.
A chevron – see? – across your mighty breast.'

   And then to me: 'He stands his own accuser.      76
It's Nimrod there. Through his sick whim
no single tongue is spoken anywhere.

   So, let him be. We'll not speak in that vein.      79
For every tongue, to him, remains the same
as his tongue is to others: quite unknown.'

   Now, turning left, we made a longer march;      82
and there (the distance of a crossbow shot)
we found a bigger ogre, fiercer still.

   Who that lord was I cannot tell, who locked      85
these shackles round him and about. He held
his right arm bound in front, his left behind,

   by one tight chain that – tangling down – was hitched      88
a full five turns around the bits we saw,
netherwards stretching from his neck to waist.

   'This one, in pride, was quick to prove his power      91
against the majesty of Jupiter.'
Thus spoke my leader. 'His reward is this.

   By name Ephialtes, his deeds were done      94*
when giants caused the deities such dread.
He can't now budge the arm he wielded then.'

   And I to him: 'If it were possible      97
to gain with my own eyes experience
of measureless Briareus, *that* I'd like.'

100     'Antaeus,' he in answer said, 'you'll see
not very far from here. And he – unchained
and speaking, too – will lower us to sin's last floor.

103     The one whom you so keenly wish to see
is over there, a good way further on,
constrained like these but fiercer still in mien.'

106     No earthquake, rude in vigour, ever struck
a tower with such great force as Ephialtes,
writhing round suddenly, now shook himself.

109     And, more than ever now in mortal fear,
sheer terror would have done the trick, had I
not seen the fetters that restrained him there.

112     And now, as we proceeded on our way,
we came upon Antaeus, rising high
(omitting head) five yards above the pit.

115     'You there! Yes, you! In that propitious vale
where Hannibal turned tail with all his men –
and so made Scipio the heir of fame –

118     you brought as spoils a thousand lions back.
And if, like all your brothers, you had joined
in battle with the gods above, then (some

121     believe) those earthborn sons might well have won.
Then set us down – and please, no dark disdain –
deep in Cocytus, locked by freezing keys.

124     Don't make us trudge to Tityos or Typhon.
This man can give you what you yearn to have.
Therefore bend down. And do not twist your snout.

127     To earth he can still carry back your name.
He's living still – and so expects to, long,
unless grace summons him before his time.'

130     My teacher spoke. The giant in great haste
stretched out his hands – whose powerful clutch had once
been felt by Hercules – to take him in his fist.

133     And Virgil, when he felt himself well held,
now said to me: 'Come here so I can take you!'
He packed us in – one bundle, him and me.

Just as the Garisenda tower, when viewed            136*
beneath its leaning side, appears to fall
if any floating cloud should pass behind,

so, too, Antaeus seemed to me, as there            139
I stood expecting him to bend. And now
I'd willingly have gone some other way.

Yet lightly he set us, lightly, in those depths            142
that eat at Lucifer and Judas, too.
He did not, bowing so, make long delay,

but swayed again up straight as ship masts do.            145

# CANTO 32

1*      If I had rhymes that rawly rasped and cackled
(and chimed in keeping with that cacky hole
at which, point down, all other rock rings peak),

4      I might then squeeze the juices of my thought
more fully out of me. But since I don't,
not without dread, I bring myself to speak.

7      It's not (no kidding) any sort of joke
to form in words the universal bum,
no task for tongues still whimpering 'Mum!' and 'Dad!'

10*      The Muses, though, may raise my verse – women
who once helped Amphion lock Thebes in walls –
so fact and word may not too far diverge.

13*      You ill-begotten zombies, worst of all,
who stand there where to utter is so hard,
better had you been born as sheep or bezoars!

16      Now deep within the darkness of that well
and further even than those giant feet,
I stood and gazed sheer upwards at that wall

19      when, out of nowhere, I heard: 'Watch your step!
Don't plant those feet of yours on some poor head;
we're here all brothers in this sorry crowd.'

22      I turned at this, and now could see – around,
and all beneath, my feet – a lake of ice
that seemed far less like water than clear glass.

25      The Danube, even in winter Österreich,
never congealed its currents to so thick
a veil (the Don, neither, under freezing skies)

as this. And if the crags of Tambernic      28*
had crashed down here – or Pike Pietrapana –
its very fringe would not have cracked or creaked.

As frogs sit croaking in the harvest month      31
(when country girls will dream of gleaning corn),
their snouts just poking from the water line,

so too these shadows, fixed in ice lead-blue,      34
to where, in shame, we start to blush, their teeth
as rhythmic, beakily, as chattering storks.

And each one kept his face bent down. From mouths      37
the cold, from hearts their miseries force
a public testament to suffering.

I stood a while just gazing all around,      40*
then, glancing to my feet, I saw here two
embraced so closely that their head hair mixed.

'Go on,' I said, 'so tell me who you are,      43
straining so tightly, tit to tit.' Coupled,
the two eased back their necks. Their faces now

were straight to mine. Once moist within, their eyes      46
welled up. The teardrops flowed toward their lips.
But chill gripped these, to lock them in their holes.

To wood wood never has been clamped so hard      49
as these two were; and, overwhelmed with ire,
each butted each like any pair of goats.

Another in the frost had lost both ears.      52
Still gazing downwards, he was first to speak:
'Why eye us so, as though we were your mirror?

If you're so keen to know who these two are,      55
that valley where Bisenzio streams down
belonged to them, as to their father, earlier.

They issued from a single womb. And you      58*
may go, if you so please, through all of Cain
finding no shadow freeze in aspic fitter,

not Mordred, even – breast and shadow pierced      61*
by thrusts his "uncle", great King Arthur, gave –
neither Focaccia (source of strife), nor this one here,

64  whose head, annoyingly, so cramps my view.
His name was Sassolo Mascheroni,
and you, if you are Tuscan, know him well.

67  However, not to drag out speeches further,
be told that I'm Camiscion de' Pazzi.
I wait for Carlin. He'll acquit me here.'

70*  And then I saw a thousand mongrel faces
bitten by frost. (I shiver, remembering –
and always will – to see a frozen puddle.)

73  Trembling, as ever, in the endless nip,
onwards we went to reach the cone's last core,
where all the weight of everything weighs down.

76  And whether by intention, chance or fate
(well, I don't know!) pacing among these heads,
hard in the face of one, I struck my foot.

79  It screeched out, whingingly: 'Why stamp on me?
Unless, of course, you're here to take revenge
for Montaperti. If not, why do me harm?'

82  I to my teacher: 'Wait a little here.
I'll go and free myself of doubts with him.
Then push me on as much as you desire.'

85  My leader paused. And, turning to the one
still spitting curses out, I now inquired:
'So who are you, to go on scolding others?'

88  'And who are you? You trek through Antenora,
bashing,' he said, 'at other people's cheeks.
Were you alive, I wouldn't stand for it.'

91  'I am alive,' I answered him. 'How dear to you
I might become, if fame is what you thirst for!
I could well note your name among the rest.'

94  'I yearn,' he answered, 'for the opposite.
Just go away and give me no more grief.
You don't know how to flatter in a bog like this.'

97  And so I grasped him tight against the scalp.
'You'll name yourself,' I said to him. 'If not,
you'll find no single bristle on your topknot.'

'Don't think,' he said, 'because you pluck my curls,      100
I mean to say or show you bugger all,
bomb as you may my skull ten thousand times.'

    I'd got him twisted in my fingers now,      103
and had, already, yanked out several tufts.
He barked, but kept his eyes held firmly down.

    Another yelling now: 'What's with you, Big Mouth?      106
Not satisfied to castanet cold jaws?
You bark as well. What devil's got to you?'

    And then I said: 'I'd have you speak no more.      109
You're vile, you traitor. I'll augment your shame,
I'll carry in your name a true report.'

    'Go on,' he answered, 'gossip all you like.      112
But don't, if you get out of here, be silent
concerning him, his tongue so slick.

    He weeps for having fingered French-y silver.      115
Now you can say: "I saw that man from Duera.
He dwells where all the sinners keep quite cool."

    And should you ask me: "Are there others here?"      118
Beside you, there is Abbot Beccheria,
the one whose gizzard Florence sawed right through.

    Then Ghibelline Jack, I guess, is further on,      121
with Ganelon and Tebaldello, too.
He slid the doors of sleeping Faience back.'

    By now we had already gone our way.      124*
But then I saw two frozen in one single hole,
one head a headpiece to the one below.

    As bread is mangled by some famished mouth,      127
so too the higher gnawed the lower head,
precisely where the nape and brainstem meet.

    The dying Tydeus in this same way,      130
in loathing, chewed the brows of dead Menalippus,
gnawing the skull and everything besides.

    'O you who by so bestial a show      133
make known your hatred for the one you eat,
now tell me – why? I give my word,' I said,

136    'if you complain of him with proper cause,
       then once I know his name and how he sinned,
       I'll make you in the world a fair return,
139        provided means of speech do not fall dry.'

# CANTO 33

Jaws lifted now from that horrible dish,                               1
the sinner – wiping each lip clean on hair that fringed
the mess he'd left the head in, at its rear –

began: 'You ask that I should tell anew                                4
the pain that hopelessly, in thought alone,
before I voice it, presses at my heart.

Yet if I may, by speaking, sow the fruit                               7
of hate to slur this traitor, caught between my teeth,
then words and tears, you'll see, will flow as one.

Who you might be, I do not know, nor how                               10
you've come to be down here. But when you speak,
you seem (there's little doubt) a Florentine.

You need to see: I was Count Ugolino.                                  13*
This is Ruggieri, the archbishop, there.
I'll tell you now why we two are so close.

That I, in consequence of his vile thoughts,                           16
was captured – though I trusted in this man –
and after died, I do not need to say.

But this cannot have carried to your ears:                             19
that is, how savagely I met my death.
You'll hear it now, and know if he has injured me.

One scant slit in the walls of Eaglehouse                              22*
(because of me, they call it now the Hunger Tower.
Be sure, though: others will be locked up there)

had shown me, in the shaft that pierces it,                            25
many new moons by now, when this bad dream
tore wide the veil of what my future was.

28*    This thing here then appeared to me as Master
       of the Hounds, who tracked the wolf – his cubs as well –
       out on the hill where Lucca hides from Pisa.

31     In front, as leaders of the pack, he placed
       the clans Gualandi, Sismond and Lanfranchi,
       their bitches hunting eager, lean and smart.

34     The chase was brief. Father and sons, it seemed,
       were wearying; and soon – or so it seemed –
       I saw those sharp fangs raking down their flanks.

37     I woke before the day ahead had come,
       and heard my sons (my little ones were there)
       cry in their sleep and call out for some food.

40     How hard you are if, thinking what my heart
       foretold, you do not feel the pain of it.
       Whatever will you weep for, if not that?

43     By now they all had woken up. The time
       was due when, as routine, our food was brought.
       Yet each was doubtful, thinking of their dream.

46     Listening, I heard the door below locked shut,
       then nailed in place against that dreadful tower.
       I looked in their dear faces, spoke no word.

49     I did not weep. Inward, I turned to stone.
       They wept. And then my boy Anselmo spoke:
       "What are you staring at? Father, what's wrong?"

52     And so I held my tears in check and gave
       no answer all that day, nor all the night
       that followed on, until another sun came up.

55     A little light had forced a ray into
       our prison, so full of pain. I now could see
       on all four faces my own expression.

58     Out of sheer grief, I gnawed on both my hands.
       And they – who thought I did so from an urge
       to eat – all, on the instant, rose and said:

61     "Father, for us the pain would be far less
       if you would chose to eat us. You, having dressed us
       in this wretched flesh, ought now to strip it off."

So I kept still, to not increase their miseries.     64
And that day and the day beyond, we all were mute.
Hard, cruel earth, why did you not gape wide?

As then we reached the fourth of all those days,     67
Gaddo pitched forward, stretching at my feet.
"Help me," he said. "Why don't you help me, Dad!"

And there he died. You see me here. So I saw them,     70
the three remaining, falling one by one
between the next days – five and six – then let

myself, now blind, feel over them, calling     73
on each, now all were dead, for two days more.
Then hunger proved a greater power than grief.'

His words were done. Now, eyes askew, he grabbed     76
once more that miserable skull – his teeth,
like any dog's teeth, strong against the bone.

Pisa, you scandal of the lovely land     79*
where 'yes' is uttered in the form of *sì*,
your neighbours may be slow to punish you,

but let those reefs, Capraia and Gorgogna,     82
drift, as a barrage, to the Arno's mouth,
so that your people – every one – are drowned.

So what if – as the rumour goes – the great Count     85
Ugolino did cheat fortresses from you.
You had no right to crucify his children.

Pisa, you are a newborn Thebes! Those boys     88
were young. That made them innocent. I've named
just two. I now name Uguiccione and Brigata.

We now moved on, and came to where the ice     91
so roughly swaddled yet another brood.
And these – not hunched – bend back for all to view.

They weep. Yet weeping does not let them weep.     94
Their anguish meets a blockage at the eye.
Turned in, this only makes their heartache more.

Their tears first cluster into frozen buds,     97
and then – as though a crystal visor – fill
the socket of the eye beneath each brow.

100    My own face now – a callus in the chill –
       had ceased to be a throne to any kind
       of sentiment. And yet, in spite of all,

103    it seemed I felt a wind still stirring here.
       'Who moves these currents, sir?' I now inquired.
       'At depths like these, aren't vapours wholly spent?'

106    He in reply: 'Come on, come on! You soon
       will stand where your own probing eye shall see
       what brings this drizzling exhalation on.'

109    A case of icy-eye-scab now yelled out:
       'You must be souls of such malignancy
       you merit placement in the lowest hole.

112    Prise off this rigid veil, to clear my eyes.
       Let me awhile express the grief that swells
       in my heart's womb before my tears next freeze.'

115    I answered: 'Are you asking help from me?
       Tell me who you are. Then I'll free your gaze,
       or travel – promise! – to the deepest ice.'

118*   'I,' he replied, 'am Brother Alberigo,
       I of the Evil Orchard, Fruiterer.
       Here I receive exquisite dates for figs.'

121    'Oh,' I now said, 'so you're already dead?'
       'Well, how my body fares above,' he said,
       'still in the world, my knowledge is not sure.

124*   There is, in Ptolomea, this advantage,
       that souls will frequently come falling down
       before Fate Atropos has granted them discharge.

127    I very willingly will tell you more,
       but only scrape this tear-glaze from my face.
       The instant any soul commits, like me,

130    some act of treachery, a demon takes
       possession of that body-form and rules
       its deeds until its time is done. Swirling,

133*   the soul runs downwards to this sink. And so
       the body of that shade behind – a-twitter
       all this winter through – still seems up there, perhaps.

You're bound to know, arriving only now,    136
that this is Signor Branca ("Hookhand") d'Oria.
Years have gone by since he was ice-packed here.'

    'I think,' I said, 'that this must be a con.    139
For how can Branca d'Oria be dead?
He eats and drinks and sleeps and puts his clothes on.'

    'Recall that ditch,' he said, 'named Rotklorsville,    142
where, higher up, they brew adhesive pitch?
Well, long before Mike Zanche got to that,

    Hookhand was history. He, as proxy, left    145
a devil in his skin (his kinsman's here as well,
the one who planned with him the double-cross).

    But please, now reach your hand to me down here.    148
Open my eyes for me.' I did not open them.
To be a swine in this case was pure courtesy.

    You Genovese, deviant, deranged    151
and stuffed with every sort of vicious canker!
Why have you not been wiped yet from the earth?

    Among the worst of all the Romagnuoli    154
I found there one of yours, whose works were such
his soul already bathes in Cocytus.

    His body, seemingly, lives on above.    157

# CANTO 34

1*     '*Vexilla regis prodeunt inferni*,
marching towards us. Fix your eyes ahead,'
my teacher said, 'and see if you can see it.'

4     As though a windmill when a thick fog breathes –
or else when dark night grips our hemisphere –
seen from a distance, turning in the wind,

7      so there a great contraption had appeared.
And I now shrank, against the wind, behind
my guide. There were no glades to shelter in.

10     I was by now (I write this verse in fear)
where all the shades in ice were covered up,
transparent as are straws preserved in glass.

13     Some lay there flat, and some were vertical,
one with head raised, another soles aloft,
another like a bow, bent face to feet.

16     And then when we had got still further on,
where now my master chose to show to me
that creature who had once appeared so fair,

19     he drew away from me and made me stop,
saying: 'Now see! Great Dis! Now see the place
where you will need to put on all your strength.'

22     How weak I now became, how faded, dry –
reader, don't ask, I shall not write it down –
for anything I said would fall far short.

25     I neither died nor wholly stayed alive.
Just think yourselves, if your minds are in flower,
what I became, bereft of life and death.

The emperor of all these realms of gloom    28*
stuck from the ice at mid-point on his breast.
And I am more a giant (to compare)
    than any giant measured to his arm.    31
So now you'll see how huge the whole must be,
when viewed in fit proportion to that limb.

    If, once, he was as lovely as now vile,    34
when first he raised his brow against his maker,
then truly grief must all proceed from him.

    How great a wonder it now seemed to me    37
to see three faces on a single head!
The forward face was bright vermilion.

    The other two attached themselves to that    40
along each shoulder on the central point,
and joined together at the crest of hair.

    The rightward face was whitish, dirty yellow.    43
The left in colour had the tint of those
beyond the source from which the Nile first swells.

    Behind each face there issued two great vanes,    46
all six proportioned to a fowl like this.
I never saw such size in ocean sails.

    Not feathered as a bird's wings are, bat-like    49
and leathery, each fanned away the air,
so three unchanging winds moved out from him,

    Cocytus being frozen hard by these.    52
He wept from all six eyes. And down each chin
both tears and bloody slobber slowly ran.

    In every mouth he mangled with his teeth    55
(as flax combs do) a single sinning soul,
but brought this agony to three at once.

    Such biting, though, affects the soul in front    58
as nothing to the scratching he received.
His spine at times showed starkly, bare of skin.

    'That one up there, condemned to greater pain,    61
is Judas Iscariot,' my teacher said,
'his head inside, his feet out, wriggling hard.

64*    The other two, their heads hung down below,
       are Brutus, dangling from the jet black snout
       (look how he writhes there, uttering not a word!),
67         the other Cassius with burly look.
       But night ascends once more. And now it's time
       for us to quit this hole. We've seen it all.'

70         As he desired, I clung around his neck.
       With purpose, he selected time and place
       and, when the wings had opened to the full,

73         he took a handhold on the furry sides,
       and then, from tuft to tuft, he travelled down
       between the shaggy pelt and frozen crust.

76         But then, arriving where the thigh bone turns
       (the hips extended to their widest there),
       my leader, with the utmost stress and strain,

79         swivelled his head to where his shanks had been
       and clutched the pelt like someone on a climb,
       so now I thought: 'We're heading back to Hell.'

82         'Take care,' my teacher said. 'By steps like these,'
       breathless and panting, seemingly all-in,
       'we need to take our leave of so much ill.'

85         Then through a fissure in that rock he passed
       and set me down to perch there on its rim.
       After, he stretched his careful stride towards me.

88         Raising my eyes, I thought that I should see
       Lucifer where I, just now, had left him,
       but saw instead his legs held upwards there.

91         If I was struggling then to understand,
       let other dimwits think how they'd have failed
       to see what point it was that I now passed.

94         'Up on your feet!' my teacher ordered me.
       'The way is long, the road is cruelly hard.
       The sun is at the morning bell already.'

97         This was no stroll, where now we had arrived,
       through any palace but a natural cave.
       The ground beneath was rough, the light was weak.

'Before my roots are torn from this abyss,                    100
sir,' I said, upright, 'to untangle me
from error, say a little more of this.

Where is the ice? And why is that one there            103*
fixed upside down? How is it that the sun
progressed so rapidly from evening on to day?'

And he in answer: 'You suppose you're still              106
on that side of the centre where I gripped
that wormrot's coat that pierces all the world.

While I was still descending, you were there.           109
But once I turned, you crossed, with me, the point
to which from every part all weight drags down.

So you stand here beneath the hemisphere            112
that now is covered wholly with dry land,
under the highest point at which there died

the one man sinless in his birth and life.                 115
Your feet are set upon a little sphere
that forms the other aspect of Giudecca.

It's morning here. It's evening over there.               118
The thing that made a ladder of his hair
is still as fixed as he has always been.

Falling from Heaven, when he reached this side,    121
the lands that then spread out to southern parts
in fear of him took on a veil of sea.

These reached our hemisphere. Whatever now     124
is visible to us – in flight perhaps from him –
took refuge here and left an empty space.'

There is a place (as distant from Beelzebub           127
as his own tomb extends in breadth)
known not by sight but rather by the sound

of waters falling in a rivulet                                   130
eroding, by the winding course it takes (which is
not very steep), an opening in that rock.

So now we entered on that hidden path,                133
my lord and I, to move once more towards
a shining world. We did not care to rest.

136       We climbed, he going first and I behind,
until through some small aperture I saw
the lovely things the skies above us bear.

139       Now we came out, and once more saw the stars.

# Notes

For each canto in these notes, the reader will find broadly factual information and cross-references to texts cited by Dante that are worth reading alongside Dante's own. The asterisks in the poem text show the beginning of the *terzina* to which such a note applies. Sometimes this points to a sequence of *terzine* in which, by consolidating these references, readers may discern some pattern of concerns – with, say, the minutiae of thirteenth-century politics – that will better emerge than in a strictly line-by-line treatment. Where an indeterminate number of *terzine* are covered by a note, the first line number is cued along with 'f' ('following [lines]') to indicate that a substantial section of the canto may be included. Fuller commentary on the text may be found in the three-volume edition of this translation of *The Divine Comedy* – also published in Penguin Classics (London, 2006–7) and containing Dante's original Italian text – from which the notes here have been compiled. This edition attempts to disturb as little as possible the reader's enjoyment of the narrative flow of Dante's poem. Traditional annotations in sequential form are to be found in the excellent editions by Robert Durling and Ronald Martinez (Oxford, 1996) and the well-conceived apparatus by David Higgins in his commentary on C. H. Sissons's translation (London, 1980). To both of these editions the present editor is glad to acknowledge a warm debt of gratitude. Quotes from the Bible are from the Authorized Version.

## INFERNO

### CANTO 1

*The dark wood and the sunlit hill. The appearance of Virgil. The beginning of the path down through Hell.*

160 NOTES TO INFERNO: CANTO I

1–6 Biblical references to the span of human life as threescore years
and ten are to be found in Psalm 90: 10, which Dante quotes in
*Convivio* 4, where he discourses at length on the four ages of
human life and the characteristics proper to each of them. The
notion of a road of righteousness is contained in Psalm 23, along
with that of the 'valley' of death. Isaiah 38: 10 reads: 'in the cut-
ting off of my days I shall go to the gates of the grave'. The wood
recalls the Romance wood that in, say, Arthurian legend the hero
may encounter in his search for the Holy Grail.

13–18 The hill is a figure for hope in Psalms 24: 3, 43: 3 and 121: 1.

28–30 Dante's obscure reference to his 'firm foot' has provoked much
discussion. The best explanation is that he has in mind Aris-
totle's observation that our stride is led by the *right* foot, leaving
the *left* foot to impel our movement forwards. The line may also
be taken as an example of the extreme precision of mind which
leads Dante to note exactly where, in any narrative scene, his
own body is placed and what lies to left and right of him.

31–60 The three beasts seem to be drawn from Jeremiah 5: 6, an Old
Testament book to which Dante showed particular devotion.
Allegorically, the leopard has been taken to represent false (and
possibly sexual) pleasure, which fascinates but also irritates the
mind. The lion may stand for pride, haughty but in reality a dan-
gerous void. The wolf may be taken as avarice and is of particular
importance, being the only beast of the three to which Dante
refers in his appeal to Virgil. (See also *Purgatorio* 20: 10–12.)
Avarice, for Dante, characterizes the corrupt culture of capitalist
Florence, and is above all a pointless and never-ending pursuit of
false and unsatisfying goods. In this sense it is a '*bestia sanza
pace*' ('brute which knows no peace' (line 58)), a restlessness of
mind that erodes the harmony of civic life.

64–6 Though Dante, without yet realizing it, is speaking to a pagan
figure, he invokes here the great penitential psalm '*Miserere
Domine*' (Psalm 51: 1): 'Have mercy upon me, O God, accord-
ing to thy lovingkindness: according unto the multitude of thy
tender mercies blot out my transgressions.'

67–75 Virgil (70 BC–19 BC) links his own success as a poet with the
major themes of his narrative in the *Aeneid*, which tells of the
fall of Troy (Ilion being its great citadel), the travels of Aeneas
and the foundation of Rome as a new homeland (lines 106–8)
which achieves imperial glory under Augustus. Virgil will act as
Dante's guide and companion until his disappearance in *Purga-
torio* 30. In the *Inferno*, Dante is especially influenced by – and

competes with – book 6 of the *Aeneid*, which describes the descent of the epic hero Aeneas into the underworld in pursuit of prophetic vision (see especially *Inferno* 3). The *Purgatorio* pays particular attention to Virgil's pastoral poems, the *Eclogues* (see *Purgatorio* 21–2).

94–105  The 'hound' (*'veltro'*) has been variously identified as Can Grande della Scala (1291–1329), one of Dante's patrons in exile; Emperor Henry VII (*c.* 1275–1313), whom Dante hoped, vainly, would restore imperial rule to Italy; and even as Dante himself. The phrase 'between the felt and felt' may refer to geographical location (between the towns of Feltre and Montefeltro in northern Italy). The mythological Gemini, the 'twins', were thought to wear felt caps, so that anyone born under that star sign – as Dante was – would have been born 'between the felt and felt'. Scholarly ingenuity (of a kind which henceforth these notes will not indulge) can, however, all too easily diminish the imaginative impact of enigma itself. Dante is rarely enigmatic. But when he is, it is with poetic purpose.

# CANTO 2

*Virgil explains how Beatrice chose him as Dante's guide.*

1–9  These lines, like others in the canto, make liberal reference to Virgil's *Aeneid* (see also lines 127–9). Here, in delicately responsive pastiche, Dante recalls the many passages where Aeneas is left alone at night wondering how best to serve his needy companions: 'Night it was and night through every land held the weary creatures, the creatures of flight and the flocks while the father . . .' (*Aeneid* 8: 26–7). For Virgilian invocations to the Muses, see *Aeneid* 1: 1–11.

13–27  Like Virgil in *Inferno* 1, Dante adopts here an elevated circumlocutory style: the 'sire of Silvius' is Aeneas himself. Aeneas's vision in the underworld of the future glories of Rome – revealed to him by his own father, Anchises – is combined, syncretically, with a Christian vision of Rome's future. Cf., as a parallel to the meeting of Aeneas and Anchises, Dante's own meeting with his forefather Cacciaguida in *Paradiso* 15–17.

28–30  Like Aeneas, Saint Paul – while still in his human body – was granted a vision of divine glory:

> I knew a man in Christ above fourteen years ago, (whether in the body, I cannot tell; or whether out of the body, I cannot tell: God knoweth;) such an one caught up to the third heaven.
>
> And I knew such a man, (whether in the body, or out of the body, I cannot tell: God knoweth;)
>
> How that he was caught up into paradise, and heard unspeakable words, which it is not lawful for a man to utter.
>
> 2 Corinthians 12: 2–4

For Dante's treatment of his own bodily vision, see *Paradiso* 2: 37–9.

52–81 Beatrice, who here speaks to Virgil, is (in Dante's account) the central figure in the *Commedia*, and also of his Christian understanding. The *Vita nuova* is Dante's early account of his love for her, of the poetry he wrote in her name and of the way in which he responded to her death. An example of the style of this early poetry, which exerts a strong influence over the present passage, is the last sonnet in that work, which anticipates Dante's attention here to both universal spaces and intimate effects of emotion, to tears, sighs and the light of eyes: 'Beyond the sphere that circles most widely, / there passes the sigh that leaves my heart / a new understanding which Love, / weeping, imparts to him, draws him ever higher' (*Vita nuova* 41).

94–126 The first lady to speak in Heaven is the Virgin Mary. Dante talks of his devotion to her at *Paradiso* 23: 88, and a sustained prayer to the Blessed Virgin prepares for his vision of God in *Paradiso* 33: 1–39. Saint Lucy is the patron saint of sight. According to an anecdote in the commentary written by Dante's son Jacopo, Dante was especially devoted to this saint, and Dante himself in *Convivio* 3: 9 records how he prayed to her when his eyesight had been endangered by too much study. Saint Lucy has an important role in *Purgatorio* 9 and appears in *Paradiso* 32: 13–18. Rachel is the second wife of Jacob (Genesis 29). She was frequently regarded as a figure for contemplation, and fulfils this role in *Purgatorio* 27: 104–8. (See also *Paradiso* 32: 8–9.)


# CANTO 3

*The entry into Hell. Charon and the apathetic sinners.*

1–9 The originality of Dante's treatment of Hell may be gauged by comparing these lines (and the plan of Hell offered in *Inferno* 11) with visual representations such as Giotto's in the Scrovegni chapel at Padua or in the mosaics of the Baptistery. Where, traditionally, Hell is pictured as chaos, violence and ugliness, Dante sees a vision of terrifying order expressing the underlying structure of a world that God has created but sinners have refused to contemplate. Hell Gate is not simply an awe-inspiring threat, but a demand that intelligence and understanding should be engaged anew in the analysis and exploration of divine purpose. (See also the Plan of Hell on p. vi, and Dante's own discussion of the moral categories of Hell in *Inferno* 11.)

16–18 '[T]he good that intellect desires to win' is a phrase much influenced – as is so much of Dante's thinking – by Aristotle's *Ethics*. Aristotle writes in the *Nicomachean Ethics* 6: 2: 1139a:

> What affirmation and negation are in thinking, pursuit and avoidance are in desire; so that since moral virtue is a state of character concerned with choice, and choice is deliberate desire, therefore must the reasoning be true and the desire right, if the choice is to be good, and the latter must pursue just what the former asserts. Now this kind of intellect and of truth is practical. But of the intellect which is contemplative, not practical nor productive, the good and bad state are truth and falsity respectively . . . The origin of action . . . is choice, and that of choice is desire and reasoning with a view to an end.
>
> D. Ross (trans.), *The Nicomachean Ethics of Aristotle* (Oxford, 1954, p. 92)

(Cf. Dante, *Convivio* 4: 7, 12.)

34f For the apathetic, see Revelation 3: 15–16: 'I know thy works, that thou art neither cold nor hot: I would thou wert cold or hot. So then because thou art lukewarm, and neither cold nor hot, I will spue thee out of my mouth.'

55–7 T. S. Eliot alludes to these lines in *The Waste Land* (1922): 'Unreal City, / Under the brown fog of a winter dawn, / A crowd flowed over London Bridge, so many, / I had not thought death had undone so many' (lines 60–63). For Eliot's continuing engagement with Dante's poetry, see especially *Inferno* 27 and *Purgatorio* 26. His phrase in *Four Quartets* (1943) 'human kind / Cannot bear very much reality' accurately interprets Dante's thinking about the apathetic.

58–60 The apathetic are unlike almost all other sinners in Hell in being unnamed. It is a mark of particular contempt for their wasted lives that names should be denied them. It is, however, generally accepted that Dante refers here to Pietro da Morrone (1215–96), who became Pope Celestine V in 1294, rather than other candidates such as Pontius Pilate or Judas Iscariot. History (if not Dante) speaks well of Celestine. A saintly figure, known to be a spiritual reformer who founded the Order of Celestines, he was canonized shortly after his death. But the 'great denial', which in Dante's eyes seems to have damned him, was his abdication after only five months, under pressure from the Curia and his successor, Boniface VIII (c. 1235–1303). This act of *viltà* (or cowardice) put an end to the possibility of reform, and opened the way to the election of the pope whom Dante hated and despised above all others. (For Boniface, see especially *Inferno* 19.)

82–111 Dante offers an animated variation on Virgil's treatment of Charon: 'A terrifying ferryman is guardian of these waters. His filth is fearsome; his chin is covered with a thick straggle of grey whiskers; his eyes are flames' (*Aeneid* 6: 298–300).

112–14 As at *Inferno* 2: 127–9, Dante deliberately alludes to the *Aeneid* 6: 309–12 and suggests the measure of both his stylistic and moral differences from Virgil. Milton makes comparable use of the autumn leaf simile in *Paradise Lost* 1.


# CANTO 4

*The First Circle of Hell. Limbo. Unbaptized children.*
*Virtuous pagans.*


46–63 The Harrowing of Hell – when Christ entered Hell and broke open its gates on Easter Saturday – brought salvation to those among the Hebrew patriarchs who had anticipated or prophesied Christ's coming, but not to the noble pagan. This event is also much in Dante's mind in *Inferno* 12 and 21–2. Attention is drawn here to Jacob (named Israel), father of the twelve tribes of Israel, who served fourteen years to win the hand of Rachel. (See Genesis 29: 9f; also *Purgatorio* 27: 100–11.)

88–90 Of the four classical poets who welcome Dante and Virgil, Homer alone was unavailable to Dante, who knew no Greek. But Dante did know of his reputation through his reading of Cicero, Virgil and other Latin poets; and in canto 26 of the *Inferno* he offers his own, highly revisionary account of the Odysseus legend. The other three are Quintus Horatius Flaccus (65–8 BC), Publius Ovidius Naso (43 BC–c. AD 17) and Marcus Annaeus Lucanus (AD 39–65). The influence of all these poets upon Dante's *Commedia* is evident at later points, notably in *Inferno* 25, where Dante claims he can outdo anything that Ovid and Lucan can achieve.

121–9 This Electra is not the daughter of Agamemnon but of Atlas. As the mother of Dardanus, one of the legendary founders of Troy, she occupies a legitimate position – alongside Hector, Aeneas and Julius Caesar – among the heroes of the Trojan line which eventually founded Rome. Camilla and Penthesilea, queen of the Amazons, are both virgin warriors mentioned by Virgil (*Aeneid* 1: 490–93, 7: 803–17 and 11: 648–835). The former was supposed to be an ally of Latinus, the latter of the Trojans. Brutus and Cornelia, as figures in Roman history, were known to Dante from Livy, Lucan and others. Brutus was first consul of the Roman republic after the expulsion of the kings. Lucrece or Lucretia, wife of Collatinus, committed suicide after being raped by the son of King Tarquin. Julia, daughter of Julius Caesar, married Pompey the Great, who later became her father's greatest enemy. For Marcia, wife of Cato of Utica, see *Purgatorio* 1. Cornelia was the wife of Scipio Africanus. Saladdin (Salah ad-Din, 1137–93), sultan of Egypt, drove the Crusaders out of the Holy Land. But many legends concerning his heroism and generosity proliferated in the west.

130–44 The 'master of all those who think and know' is Aristotle (384–322 BC). Dante knew about Plato (427–347 BC) and his treatment of Socrates through Latin texts. Diogenes the Cynic (fourth century BC) rejected the claims of supposedly civilized existence. Anaxogoras (fifth century BC) was both philosopher and mentor of Pericles. Thales (seventh century BC) was considered the founder of Greek philosophy. Empedocles of Sicily (fifth century BC) was both a rhetorician and the inventor of the notion of the four elements. Heraclitus of Ephesus (fifth century BC) held that fire was the fundamental element. Zeno of Citium (third century BC) is praised by Dante in *Convivio* 4, and is considered the founder of the Stoic school. Dioscorides of Anazarbus (first century AD) founded pharmacology. Orpheus and Linus are mythical poets. Tullius is Marcus Tullius Cicero (106–43 BC), Roman statesman and philosopher, whose *De Amicitia* and *De Officiis* were acknowledged influences on Dante's thought. Seneca (d. AD 65) influenced Dante through his Stoic philosophy.

Euclid (fourth century BC) is the Greek geometrician. Ptolemy of Alexandria (second century AD) devised the astronomical system, posited on a geocentric universe, that Dante adopts in imagining the universe of the *Commedia* (see P. Boyde, *Dante, Philomythes and Philosopher* (Cambridge, 1981)). Hippocrates (fourth century BC) founded medical studies. Avicenna (d. 1036) was an Arabic physician and philosopher. Galen of Pergamum (second century AD) wrote medical textbooks. Averroes (d. 1198) was one of the most important philosophers of the Middle Ages. Born in Arabic Spain – his name in Arabic is Ibn Rushd – his great commentary on Aristotle won him the name of 'the commentator' (see also *Purgatorio* 25: 63–5). Scholasticism – and Dante – owed much to his influence, even if inclined to resist its implications.

# CANTO 5

*Minos, judge of the underworld. The lustful.*
*Francesca da Rimini.*

4–6 In classical legend, Minos, king of Crete, is the son of Zeus and Europa. He appears as the terrifyingly sombre judge of the underworld in Virgil's *Aeneid* 6: 566–9.

52–67 Semiramis, widow of King Ninus, the legendary founder of the Babylonian Empire, was, according to Saint Augustine of Hippo, Paulus Orosius and Brunetto Latini (see *Inferno* 15), guilty of incest with her son and used her political position to make this crime legitimate. Dido, queen of Carthage, deserted the memory of her first (dead) husband Sichaeus out of love for Aeneas, but committed suicide when Aeneas left Carthage to continue his journey to Italy and found Rome. The marriage of Cleopatra, queen of Egypt, to Mark Antony precipitated a civil war between Antony and Octavius, who was to become Roman emperor. Helen of Troy was the wife of Menelaus, king of Sparta, and her abduction by Paris, son of the Trojan king Priam, led to the Trojan War. Achilles, the Greek warrior, was ready to betray his countrymen when he fell in love with Polysena, daughter of Priam, but was ambushed and killed by Paris before he could complete his act of betrayal. Tristan – in love with Iseult, wife of his uncle King Mark of Cornwall – was killed as a traitor by the king's poisoned spear.

73f Dante focuses on two figures from thirteenth-century Italian history – Francesca da Rimini, wife of Gianciotto Malatesta (marriage c. 1275), and Paolo, Gianciotto's brother. Francesca was married by political arrangement to Gianciotto, a member of the ruling family of Rimini, but began an affair (as described here) with Paolo. When he discovered this, Gianciotto murdered both his wife and his brother. This was a great scandal in its day. Remarkably, Dante, having consigned Francesca to Hell, was supported between 1317 and 1320 by the patronage of her nephew, Guido Novello da Polenta.

88f Francesca may declare at line 91 that if the Sovereign of the Universe were her friend, she would pray for Dante's peace of mind. But God, who condemns her to Hell, is not her friend; and so the prayer must fail. Likewise, the sweetness of Francesca's rhetorical repetition (in Dante's Italian original) of 'Amor' is matched by an emphasis on violent actions hidden in the second line of each of these *terzine*. Francesca displays a continuing evasiveness, seeking to shift the blame for her fate away from her own person. It is 'Love' which takes possession of her and it is the book (see lines 133–4 and 137) rather than her own passion which leads her into adultery. Thus the particularly mellifluous line 103, '*Amor, ch'a nullo amato amar perdona*' ('Love, who no loved one pardons love's requite'), reveals itself on examination to be a morally dubious justification of love as an obsessive submission to fate, in which no one who is the object of love has the right to deny love in return to the person that projects that love. On this view, Dante does not condemn Francesca for lust alone. (Among those redeemed in the *Purgatorio* and *Paradiso* are figures who submitted to lust, including the sodomites and bestialists of *Purgatorio* 26 and the courtesans and whores in *Paradiso* 8 and 9.) Her sin is rather one of moral apathy and failed intelligence.

106–7 Caina in the geography of Hell is the region in the lowest circles (see *Inferno* 32) assigned to those who, like Cain, murdered members of their kin (Genesis 4: 1–15).

121–38 Francesca and Paolo are here reading a version of *The Book of Launcelot of the Lake* (an early thirteenth-century prose account of the Arthurian legend). The 'single point' which overcame them is Lancelot confessing his love to Guinevere, under persuasion from Galehault (Galeotto in Italian). '*Galeotto*' thus came to mean the type of a go-between or pander. Note that, whereas Francesca claims to have been kissed by Paolo, Guinevere is always presented as giving the first kiss to Lancelot.

# CANTO 6

*The circle of the gluttons, guarded by Cerberus.*
*Ciacco. The politics of Florence in 1300.*

**13–32** Cerberus (like Charon in *Inferno* 3, a modification and intensification of Virgil's original) is to be found as the watchdog of Hades in *Aeneid* 6: 417–22.

**40–73** Ciacco – though a historical figure who is the subject of a lively anecdote by Giovanni Boccaccio in the *Decameron* 9: 8 – is allowed no name save a nickname which means 'porker' or 'hog' (line 52). He has no standing or stable position within the order of society; and, indeed, when he speaks of his fellow citizens, he divisively relishes the fate they will suffer. Such Schadenfreude extends even to his attitude to Dante. Through Ciacco's mouth Dante alludes for the first time to his own political exile (lines 64–84). The exchange here between the two Florentines and Dante provides a (sometimes allusive) account of the factional strife between White and Black Guelfs which came to a head around 1300–1302 and brought about Dante's exile. The Blacks had rioted in 1301 and Dante, in his role as one of the priors of Florence, had been obliged to exile members of both Black and White factions. The Whites were the 'country' party – hence 'Wildwood'; their leaders, the Cerchi, came from the rural environs of Florence – and in 1300 the Whites had won a temporary superiority. But the Blacks regrouped, and within the span of three years ('three brief suns' (line 67)) they returned to power. Their cause was supported by the 'one who now just coasts between' (line 69) – that is, Pope Boniface VIII – keeping open the option of alliance with both Blacks and Whites.

**79–84** All the great Florentines that Dante here disingenuously inquires about are found in the lower circles of Hell. Notes on Farinata can be found in *Inferno* 10, on Rusticucci and Tegghiaio in *Inferno* 16 and on Mosca in *Inferno* 28. Arrigo – whose identity cannot be determined – is not mentioned elsewhere.

**106–8** This principle is enunciated by Aristotle in the *Nicomachean Ethics* 10: 4.

**115** Plutus, the god of riches, dominates the first phase of *Inferno* 7.

# CANTO 7

*The avaricious and the spendthrift. The doctrine of*
*fortune. The wrathful and the melancholic.*

1–9  Dante imagines Plutus as a combination of the god of wealth and
the god of the underworld. Plutus's speech is impenetrable gib-
berish. At line 8, the wolf referred to recalls the she-wolf of
*Inferno* 1: 49–60 and anticipates a further reference in *Purgato-*
*rio* 20: 10.

10–12  The archangel Michael leads the attack that drives Satan from
Heaven.

22–7  Cf. Virgil, *Aeneid* 3: 420–23. Charybdis is the mythological name
for the whirlpools in the Straits of Messina. The reference to the sea
recalls Anicius Boethius's *Consolation of Philosophy* (524–5). For
Boethius, it was merchants who originally disturbed the harmony
of the Golden Age by their maritime enterprise. The punishment of
the rocks evokes the labours of Sisyphus in *Aeneid* 6: 616.

43–5  Avarice is punished alongside its opposite, prodigality. Aristotle
suggests this coupling in the *Nicomachean Ethics* 4: 1: 1121a.
Following Aristotle here, as elsewhere, Dante would identify
virtue as a mean between two vicious extremes. In this case,
liberality would constitute the virtuous mean.

73–96  This picture of Fortune draws upon but modifies the concept
developed by Boethius in the *Consolation of Philosophy*, in which
the world is subject to a constant shifting of Fortune's wheel:

> So with imperious hand she turns the wheel of change
> This way and that like the ebb and flow of the tide.
> And pitiless she tramples down those once dread kings,
> Raising the lowly face of the conquered –
> Only to mock him in his turn.
> Careless she neither hears nor heeds the cries
> Of miserable men.
>
> *Consolation of Philosophy* 1: 1

Dante, by contrast, attributes to Fortune angelic powers and a
providential function. Angels (on the understanding that Dante
offers in *Paradiso* 28) are the purest forms of created intelli-
gence, and are set as governors over the movements of the
physical cosmos.

**97–9** The reference to the stars establishes the hour as just past midnight on Good Friday.

**115–29** The swamp formed by the river Styx contains within it two groups of sinners, the wrathful and the sluggardly. (One etymology for 'Styx' suggests the word means 'sorrow', which can be taken as the source of both anger and hatred.) Again, Dante is using conceptions of the Aristotelian mean to identify anger and wrath as vicious extremes.

# CANTO 8

*The swamp of the Styx. Encounter with Filippo*
*Argenti. Arrival at the city of Dis.*

**19–24** Phlegyas is drawn (much altered) from *Aeneid* 6: 618–20, where he appears as king of Thessaly. His anger there is a response to his daughter's rape by Apollo.

**31f** In this highly problematical episode, Dante encounters a fellow Florentine, the notoriously arrogant Filippo, a member of the Black Guelf Adimari clan, which is condemned by Dante in *Paradiso* 16: 115–20. Though now so caked in mud – so full of it that it seems to flow out of him – Filippo was in life nicknamed Argenti, the Silver One, apparently because he had his horses shod in silver. Concentrated in this figure is the spirit of pride and divisiveness that Dante constantly identifies among the sources of Florentine corruption. This episode is illustrated in all its violence by Eugène Delacroix in his *Dante and Virgil in Hell* (1822), now in the Louvre.

**43–5** In the passage in Luke 11: 27–8 to which these lines allude, Christ replies by rejecting the praises offered to him.

**124–6** This refers to the gate of Hell (*Inferno* 3) which since the Harrowing of Hell has always stood open.

# CANTO 9

*Entry into Dis secured by the Messenger*
*from Heaven.*

**7–9** Because (in Italian) the verb 's'offerse' and its subject 'Tal' have no gender, this broken utterance ('Yet granted such a one . . .')

may be taken to refer to Beatrice or the Messenger from Heaven who in fact arrives to open the gate.

22–30 Dante – drawing on Lucan's *Pharsalia* 6: 507 – seems to have invented the story of Virgil's earlier journey through Hell to the depths where Judas is punished, conjured to do so by the witch Erichtho. Throughout the Middle Ages, Virgil had a reputation for witchcraft – which Dante repudiates implicitly in *Inferno* 20.

37–51 Cf. Virgil, *Aeneid* 6: 570–75. The Three Furies, or Eumenides, or Erinyes, specifically pursue those who are guilty of crimes of blood. Hecate is the queen of Hell ('empress') spoken of here.

52–4 The story of the Medusa and of her power to turn men to stone is told in Ovid's *Metamorphoses* 6: 606: 249. The Furies at line 54 show regret that they did not kill Theseus (see also notes to *Inferno* 12), when they had him in their power, and thus dissuaded other travellers from passing through Hell.

97–9 Hercules is said to have defeated and chained Cerberus, who appears in *Inferno* 6.

112–15 The Roman cemeteries at Arles, near the mouth of the river Rhône, and at Pola (now Pulj) on the Istrian peninsula.


# CANTO 10

*The heretics. Farinata and Cavalcante.*

10–12 Jehoshaphat, according to Joel 3: 2, is where the Last Judgement will be announced and conducted.

13–15 Dante speaks of the Greek philosopher Epicurus with admiration in *Convivio* 4:7: 6, but here as elsewhere (see *Inferno* 12: 40–43) resists the implications of materialist metaphysics.

22f The canto is dominated by Dante's encounter with two Florentine figures, Farinata and Cavalcante – the former a Ghibelline, the latter a Guelf – from the generation preceding Dante's own, when the tensions between the Ghibelline (pro-imperial party) and the Guelf (anti-imperial party) were at their height. Dante's family was broadly Guelf in their political orientation. These men are likely to have held heterodox views, and are associated here with those 'heretics' who believe that as 'the body dies, so too the soul' (line 15). But the conversation that unrolls concerns the divided state of Florence. In particular, Farinata degli

Uberti (d. 1264), who is the first to speak, displays a deeply patriotic, if flawed, devotion to the Florentine cause.

31–51 and 76–93 Underlying Farinata's first speech and, explicitly, his concluding speech are references to the events surrounding the battle of Montaperti, near Siena – where the battlefield is traversed by the river Arbia (line 86) and where in 1260 the Florentine Guelfs were defeated by a coalition of Tuscan Ghibellines. It was Farinata who at the subsequent war council in Empoli persuaded his allies to refrain from destroying Florence. When the Guelfs recovered their supremacy, Farinata and his descendants were excluded from the amnesties of 1280. The Uberti palace, occupying the present Piazza della Signoria in Florence, was pulled down and left in Dante's lifetime as rubble, *pour encourager les autres*.

52f It is here that Dante encounters Cavalcante de' Cavalcanti (d. *c.* 1280), a Guelf aristocrat and one-time chief magistrate of Gubbio, who was the father of Guido, Dante's closest friend in his early years as a poet.

67–9 Dante has used the past remote '*elli ebbe*' ('He once . . .'), which in Italian signifies an action in the past that has no continuing connection with the present, hence implying Guido Cavalcanti's death. Dante also gives Cavalcanti's speech a Bolognese inflection: '*lume*' ('light') here becomes '*lome*'.

97–108 Dante imagines a form of myopia by which the sinners are condemned to have no knowledge of present things and to see more clearly into the distant future than into the past.

118–20 Frederick II of Hohenstaufen (1194–1250) was a Holy Roman Emperor. The cardinal is the Ghibelline Ottaviano degli Ubaldini (d. 1273), who is said to have declared: 'If I have a soul at all, I have lost it a hundred times in the interests of the Ghibellines.'

130–32 The reference, as at line 63, is to Beatrice in Heaven.


# CANTO 11

*The plan of Hell.*


7–9 The references to Anastasius and Photinus are not entirely clear, historically or syntactically. Pope Anastasius II (d. 498) was believed by medieval historians (though not by modern scholars) to have been led into an heretical denial of the divinity of Christ by his friend Photinus, deacon of Thessalonica.

**19f** Dante enunciates, through the mouth of Virgil, some of the major philosophical principles on which the moral plan or geography of Hell has been constructed. Note that his points of reference are as frequently classical as they are Christian or Scriptural. The categories do not correspond to the familiar scheme of the Seven Capital Vices, which is reserved for the plan of the *Purgatorio*.

**22f** The three forms of sin that are treated in *Inferno* 12–33 – violence, deceit and treachery – are defined in lines 22–64. All of them – unlike the sins of appetite considered in *Inferno* 5–8 – involve a conscious and 'malicious' misdirection of human intelligence. The upper circles (visited in *Inferno* 12–17) contain various forms of violent behaviour, all of which in some way – as in gang warfare, suicide or blasphemy – set the mind against the sustaining relationship it should enjoy with others, with its own being, with nature or with God. But fraud – or, better, deceit – which underlies sins such as flattery, fallacious leadership and, ultimately, treachery – is judged by Dante to be worse than violence, in that it turns the best faculties and capacities that God has given to human beings (reason and rational speech) to destructive ends.

**25–7** Human beings share with beasts a capacity for violence. But only human beings are capable of fraud – which therefore more severely offends a higher principle. (Cf. *Convivio* 3: 2: 14–19.)

**49–51** The destruction of Sodom as an archetypal city of corruption is described in Genesis 13: 10. Cahors (a city in southern France) was notorious as a centre of money-lending and usury. Blasphemers are here included among those who commit violence.

**52–66** Fraud can only be practised against our fellow human beings, since God is omniscient. In its worst form, as treachery, fraud violates the special bonds of love and trust that have been established between particular persons (lines 61–6). Simple fraud is somewhat less heinous but still violates the relationships that exist between people by virtue of their common humanity (lines 55–60). As defined by lines 61–6, fraud of the other sort is treachery, an offence against the principle fundamental to all human order which is that we should love our neighbours.

**76–90** Citing Aristotle's *Nichomachean Ethics* 7 explains the relative leniency with which Dante treats the sins of lust, greed, avarice and anger.

**94–111** Dante insists upon the sinfulness of the practice of usury, which lay at the heart of the economic developments in thirteenth-century

Florence that he viewed with such disfavour. The Italian term '*arte*' (line 100) may be taken to mean 'intelligent and purposeful work'. In this sense, divine art creates nature. Human art, operating in the natural sphere, may and – properly – must affiliate itself harmoniously with the divine original. Usury, however, makes the artificial commodity of money itself a 'second' or parodic form of creation. Here Dante draws simultaneously on Aristotle's *Metaphysics* 12: 7 and *Physics* 2: 2, as well as Genesis 3: 19f.

112–14 References to the constellations of the Fish and the Great Wain and also to the north-west wind establish – in an 'artful' reading of the natural order – that the time on the April morning of Dante's journey is about 4 a.m.

# CANTO 12

*The Minotaur, centaurs and those who are guilty of violence against the person or possessions of others.*

4–9 These lines probably refer to the Lavini di Marco, twenty miles south of the city of Trento in northern Italy.

10–27 The Minotaur (part human, part bull) was the offspring of the union between Pasiphae, wife of King Minos of Crete, and a white bull with which she became infatuated. (Cf. *Purgatorio* 26: 40–42.) Minos ordered Daedalus to construct the labyrinth in which the Minotaur would be confined. With the aid of the Minotaur's sister, Arianna, the duke of Athens, Theseus, entered the labyrinth and slew the monster. (See Ovid, *Metamorphoses* 8: 152–82 and *The Art of Love* 2; also Virgil, *Aeneid* 6: 14–33.)

31–45 These lines alert the reader to a Christian myth, understanding of which lies beyond the world envisaged in classical legend. Here Virgil focuses (as does Dante's narrative elsewhere – for instance, *Inferno* 4 and 21–2) on the effect of divine power which – with Christ's entry into Hell on Easter Saturday – sent a great earth tremor through the region, leading to landslides and ruin in this, as in every other, circle of Hell. The tremor, however, is a redemptive power which shatters the hold exerted by human violence on humanity itself, in the restoration of universal harmony. A compressed but startling reference to this occurs at lines

40–45, where Virgil speaks of how, according to certain philosophers, any touch of love would paradoxically reduce the world to chaos. The philosophy that Virgil alludes to here is the atomistic school (representatives of which are found in Limbo at *Inferno* 4: 136–8), which maintained that the existence of created forms depended upon the constant collision of streams of atomic particles. On this view, violence is essential for the creation of all that we know. But Dante will eventually end his poem with a vision of how the harmony of the created order depends upon the 'love that moves the sun and other stars'.

55–72 The centaurs are treated at length in Ovid's *Metamorphoses* 12. Nessus is slain by Hercules when the hero finds the centaur stealing his wife Deianira. As he dies, Nessus plans his revenge, offering a shirt dipped in his own blood to Hercules's wife, declaring it to be a fitting love token for Hercules, and when later she offers him the shirt, the poisoned blood begins to consume Hercules's flesh. To maintain command over his own destiny, he builds a funeral pyre and immolates himself, thus becoming a god. In this canto of two-fold beings, there are clearly parallels to be drawn between Dante, himself painfully in search of divinity, and the demi-god Hercules.

Chiron is reputedly the wisest of the centaurs, said (in Statius's *Achilleid* 1) to be the teacher of both Hercules and Achilles. Pholus (Virgil, *Georgics* 2: 256 and Ovid, *Metamorphoses* 12: 306) is renowned for his violence. Another centaur, guilty of violent theft and also slain by Hercules, appears in *Inferno* 25: 17–33.

88 It is Beatrice – the inspiration for Dante's heroic journey and for his poem – who sings this alleluia.

106–38 This list of tyrants surveys history from the time of Dionysius of Syracuse (d. 367 BC) to Alexander the Great (356–323 BC) and Pyrrhus (319–272 BC) on to Sextus Pompeius (75–35 BC), son of Pompey the Great (106–48 BC), and Attila (d. AD 453), who was thought (incorrectly) to have destroyed the city of Florence. These remote figures are interspersed with men from the history of Europe in Dante's time. Opizzo d'Este, lord of Ferrara, who was famous for his cruelty, died in 1293 at the hand of his (probably) illegitimate son and heir, Azzo. The assassin of line 119 is Guy de Montfort (d. c. 1288), who murdered a cousin of the English king Edward I in 1271 in a church at Viterbo where the cardinals had gathered to elect a pope. Renier the Mad and Renier da Corneto were notorious brigands.

# CANTO 13

*Suicides and squanderers. Pier delle*
*Vigne – transformed into a thorn tree – tells his story*
*as later the anonymous Florentine suicide tells his.*

7–9  The Cécina is a stream and Corneto a village, in the swampy area
on the borders of Tuscany and Lazio.

25–30  Line 25 depends (in Italian) on a contorted repetition of the
verb '*credere*' ('to believe or think'). At line 30 the Italian meta-
phor ('*monchi*') refers to the 'chopping off' of human limbs.
Dante's doubts will end, chopped off like a hand at the wrist, if
he puts his hand forward to pluck a twig.

31f  This episode throughout runs parallel to that in Virgil's *Aeneid* 3:
3–65, where Aeneas encounters Polydorus, youngest son of the
Trojan king Priam, transformed into a tree.

In the suicide Pier della Vigna was one of the most important
figures in the political and cultural life of the early thirteenth
century. Born in Capua around 1200 in modest circumstances,
Piero became the spokesman and chief minister of Emperor
Frederick II (1194–1250), while also contributing, in verse and
political rhetoric, to the development of Italian as a literary lan-
guage. But in 1249 he fell victim to scandal; and though (as
Dante seems to allow at lines 73–5) innocent of any treachery to
his overlord, he was still disgraced. He appears to have commit-
ted suicide by beating his brains out against his prison walls.

In the symbolism and imagery of the canto, there are remote
references to the central stories of the Christian faith. The tree
(especially a thorn tree) points to the Crucifixion and the Crown
of Thorns, and thus to Christ's Atonement, which could have
made sense of sufferings such as Piero's. Equally, Piero's name
reminds one of the disciple Peter, who did betray or at least deny
his master (although Piero did not betray Frederick) and yet still
formed the rock of the Church.

More immediately, the wood, along with the selection of Piero
as an illustration, draws to mind the situation of the poet Dante
himself. He, too, once found himself in a dark wood; and the
wood of the suicides represents an intensified version of that
'*selva oscura*' of *Inferno* 1: 2. Like Piero, Dante suffered political
disgrace, yet could not follow Piero's desperate example. Nor, it
seems, could the poet in Dante allow himself to be content with

Piero's *poetic* example. It is typical of Piero's poetry that it should cultivate a theme of desperation and death as attributes of the experience of love, as, for instance, in the opening verses of '*Amando con fin core e con speranza*':

> Loving with loyal heart and with hope,
> I was promised by Love a greater joy
> than I deserved,
> for Love exalted me in my very heart
> And I would never be able to separate from it,
> however much I longed to do so,
> so deeply is her image imprinted in my heart,
> even though Death has parted me
> in body from her –
> Death, bitter, cruel and violent.

106–9 Early commentators objected that Dante is guilty of heresy here, in suggesting that a body can be hung, at resurrection, from a tree and hence divided from its soul.

115–23 The spendthrifts are: Arcolano da Squarcia di Riccolfo Maconi (murdered 1288 near Pieve al Toppo), who, according to Boccaccio, was a member of the Sienese 'spendthrifts' society; and Jacopo da Santo Andrea (also the victim of murder), who was, like Pier della Vigna, a member of Frederick II's court and is said in an early commentary on the *Commedia* to have set fire to his own property out of a desire to witness a good blaze.

142–50 This speech obliquely recalls legends of the violent history of Florence in the early Middle Ages. As a Roman city, Florence had been founded under the influence of Mars (its first patron). But the pagan god was displaced by the Christian Saint John, to whom the Florentine Baptistery is dedicated. Yet enough of Mars's temple remained in the city for his influence to continue. The city was destroyed, in the account given by the anonymous suicide, by Attila (in fact it was besieged by Totila in AD 410) and, traditionally, refounded by the emperor Charlemagne in 801. The suicide thus suggests that without the warlike strain in its inheritance – represented by a fragment of statuary near the river Arno – the city would not have survived.

# CANTO 14

*The blasphemers. Capaneus. The Old Man of Crete.*
*The source of the rivers of Hell.*

**13–15** Cato the Younger (95 BC–AD 46) (as described in Lucan's
*Pharsalia* 9: 382f) crossed the northern Sahara in Libya during
his campaign in support of Pompey the Great against Julius Caesar.
Further references to Lucan's account occur in *Inferno* 25.

**31–6** This reference to an incident in Alexander the Great's campaign
in India draws on Albertus Magnus's *De Meteoris* 1: 4: 8, which
in turn cites a description of this event that Alexander is said to
have written to his tutor, Aristotle.

**46f** The (apparently) heroic figure of Capaneus is drawn from Statius's
*Thebaid* 3: 605, where the mythical Greek king – laying siege
to the city of Thebes – is described as the great 'contemner' of
the gods, and is finally struck down at 10: 935–9 by Jupiter's
thunderbolt.

**55–7** 'Mongibello' or Mount Jabal (a compound of the Latin '*mons*'
and the Arabic '*jabal*', both signifying 'mountain') is the popular
name for Mount Etna. This is imagined as the smithy in which
Jupiter prepares his thunderbolts.

**79–81** The Bulicame (literally, 'the boiling thing') is the name of a
stream near Viterbo that runs red with sulphur. Early commenta-
tors said it was reserved for the prostitutes of the town to bathe in.

**94–120** Though the detail of the allegory has never been fully explained,
Dante, in constructing the image of the Old Man of Crete, draws
on a wide variety of sources. The primary one is the dream of
Nebuchadnezzar recorded in Daniel 2: 31–5, which Daniel inter-
prets as representing the successive rise and fall of world empires,
beginning with Nebuchadnezzar's own. Christian interpreters
such as Richard of Saint Victor took the dream as a representa-
tion of the corruption of humanity – the head of gold being
symbolic of the freedom of the will – and the coming of Christ.
Other sources include Ovid's *Metamorphoses* 1: 89–150, which
offers an account of the ages of gold, silver and brass, and Saint
Augustine's *The City of God* 15, which draws on the account of
the excavation of a statue in Crete offered in Pliny's *Natural His-
tory* 7: 16. Dante's own references to Crete see it as the birthplace
of Zeus/Jove (lines 100–102), where his mother Rhea had fled
to save her son from the murderous rage of his father Chronos/

Saturn. It is she who caused dances and music to be performed
to conceal the cries of her baby boy. In *Inferno* 12, the troubled
history of Crete as the realm of King Minos is recorded. Minos,
as judge of the underworld, appears in *Inferno* 5.


# CANTO 15

*The sodomites. Brunetto Latini.*

**22f** In the Guelf republic of Florence, Brunetto Latini (*c.* 1220–*c.*
1294) occupied a political and cultural position comparable to
that which Pier della Vigna held in the imperial court of Freder-
ick II. He was not – as is sometimes thought – Dante's 'old
school master', but an administrator, intellectual and one-time
exile of the first importance; and Dante seems to have had some
association with the circle that gathered around Brunetto, gain-
ing from him an interest in classical rhetoric and, perhaps,
French literature.

The elder Florentine and Dante here concern themselves – as
did Dante and the Ghibelline Farinata in *Inferno* 10 – with the
divided state of their native city and the consequences of this for
Dante's own future. (It is notable that Virgil, who is now Dante's
chosen model of political and rhetorical practice, remains silent
throughout the canto, save for a tight-lipped, sardonic interven-
tion at line 99.)

Dante would have undoubtedly agreed with some of the princi-
pal tenets of Brunetto's thinking. Thus, in his commentary on
Cicero's rhetoric writings, Brunetto writes: '*What is a city?* A city
is a coming-together of persons as one to live according to rea-
son: citizens are not those who live simply in the same community
surrounded by the same city walls but those rather who are
brought to live according to rational principle.' A city, on this
understanding, is not merely a marketplace or defensive strong-
hold but the expression of common interest in rational values.
Dante's own devotion to the life of a small city, understood in
such terms, persists into *Paradiso* 8 and, especially, 15–17. It is
even possible that Brunetto's writing suggested to Dante the
ways in which he might begin his quest in the dark wood. For
Brunetto – himself suffering exile – had written in his vernacular
verse allegory *Tesoretto* (lines 190–94) of how in 'a dark wood,

coming back to conscious mind', he turned his thoughts to the ascent of a great mountain. (Cf. *Inferno* 1: 1–18.) But Brunetto would not be in Hell if, in some way, he had not failed to live up to the principles that he expresses here. He has been displaced as teacher, in respect of civic understanding, companionship and intellectual exploration, by the figure of the Roman Virgil.

61–3   The legend (recorded in Brunetto's *Livres dou Trésor* 1: 37: 1–2 and also in Giovanni Villani's *Cronica* 1: 37–8 (*c.* 1322)) is that the hilltown of Fiesole was a hotbed of revolt against Rome during the Catiline conspiracy of 62 BC and was razed to the ground by Julius Caesar. Florence was then founded in the valley as a loyal imperial colony, while the remnants of the original Fiesoleans gathered themselves over the centuries in continuing opposition to the native inhabitants whom Dante considered to be the 'sacred seed of Rome' (line 76). (Cf. *Inferno* 16 and *Paradiso* 15–17.)

106–14   The charge of sodomy was commonly levelled against intellectuals and academics, as in the important medieval text *De Planctu Naturae* (1160–70) by Alain de Lille. But Brunetto is known to have spoken out against sodomy and no direct charge is laid against him in this canto. Dante's silence here has led critics to look for a variety of other ways in which Brunetto may be thought to have committed a sin against divinely created nature.

Priscian (*fl.* 491–518) was the author of the most influential Latin grammar of the Middle Ages. Francesco d'Accorso (1225–93), doctor of civil law, acted as counsellor to the English king Edward I. Andrea de' Mozzi (d. 1296), member of an important banking family in Florence, was appointed bishop of that city in 1287; when accused of various abuses, he was transferred by Pope Boniface VIII (see *Inferno* 19 and 27) from Florence (the Arno) to Vicenza (identified in the Italian text by the river Bacchiglione which runs through it). Boniface is here ironically given the traditional appellation of the popes: '*servus servorum*' ('Slave of Slaves').

118–20   In his *Tesoretto* Brunetto writes: 'I send and present to you this rich Treasure worth its weight in silver and gold.'

121–3   The race is a *palio* for naked athletes, run in the environs of Verona on the first Sunday in Lent.

# CANTO 16

*The sodomites continued. The Guelf nobles.*
*The call to Geryon.*

37–44  Guido Guerra (1220–72) came from the noble family of the
Conti Guidi and was leader of the Tuscan Guelfs. He was the
grandson of Gualdrada di Bellincione Berti de' Ravagnani, who
is mentioned, along with her husband, in the great account of
Florence in her golden age that Dante offers in *Paradiso* 15: 97–9.
His companions in sodomy are the Guelf aristocrat Tegghiaio
Aldobrandi (d. before 1266) and the minor nobleman Iacopo
Rusticucci (*fl.* 1235–66). The words that 'ought to have more
pleased the world' are a speech he made to dissuade the Floren-
tines from engaging in the battle of Montaperti. (Cf. Farinata in
*Inferno* 10: 88–93.) The presence of all these figures in Hell was
first announced by Ciacco in *Inferno* 6.

70–73  Nothing is known of Guglielmo Borsiere, save for the picture
of his courtesy and generosity that Boccaccio offers in *Decam-
eron* 1: 8.

94–102  Here, as frequently, Dante displays the exact knowledge of
landscape that he no doubt acquired in the course of his exile.

106–114  The significance of this episode has never been satisfactorily
explained. Though Dante declares that he had once sought to
lasso the *lonza*, or leopard, of *Inferno* 1 with this cord, there is
no mention of it there. (In *Purgatorio* 1 Dante girds himself
again with a reed.) A great variety of interpretations have been
offered – the most convincing of which suggests (none too con-
vincingly) that Dante may have had some association with the
Franciscan Order, whose corded belts might be taken to signify
chastity.

# CANTO 17

*The usurers. The descent on the back of Geryon*
*to lower Hell.*

4f  Geryon (only named at line 97) originally was one of the monsters
overcome by Hercules (see Virgil, *Aeneid* 6: 288). Yet Dante here

draws equally upon Revelation, where Satan, scorpion-like, horse-like, rises out of the abyss (9: 2–7):

> And [the fifth angel] opened the bottomless pit; and there arose a smoke out of the pit, as the smoke of a great furnace ... And there came out of the smoke locusts upon the earth: and unto them was given power, as the scorpions of the earth have power ... And the shapes of the locusts were like unto horses prepared unto battle; and on their heads were as it were crowns like gold, and their faces were as the faces of men.

From this point on, the *Inferno* in its imagery and religious thinking continues to refer to the Apocalypse as depicted in Revelation. The imagery and punishments from *Inferno* 18 to 30 often reflect the images of disaster that will appear in the days preceding the Last Judgement: fire (26–7); war (28); disease (29–30).

16–18 In Ovid's *Metamorphoses* 6: 1–145, a Lydian girl, Arachne, challenges the goddess Athene to a weaving contest and, losing, is transformed into a spider. (Cf. *Purgatorio* 12: 43–5.)

58–73 Identified by their armorial bearings these figures are members of the following families: the Yellow Purse – the Gianfigliazzi, of Florence Guelfs, becoming Black Guelfs after 1300; the White Goose – the aristocratic Florentine Ghibelline Obriachi; the Blue Sow ('*scrofa*') – the Scrovegni of Padua; the Three Goats – the Florentine Buiamonte, of whom Giovanni di Buiamonte de' Becchi became Gonfaloniere (chief of police) in 1293.

106–11 Phaeton, driving the chariot of the sun, loses the reins in terror at the sight of the constellation of Scorpio (Ovid, *Metamorphoses* 2: 200), while (*Metamorphoses* 8: 226) Icarus, climbing towards the sun, finds that his wax wings melt.

# CANTO 18

*The plan of Malebolge where deceit is punished.*
*Pimps, seducers and flatterers.*

1 The invented word 'Rottenpockets' here translates the word that Dante himself invents to describe this region of Hell, '*Malebolge*' ('Evil Pockets'). *Inferno* 18–30 describe the ten '*bolge*', or 'pockets',

that contain the various sinners of deceit 'against those who
have no cause to trust'.

28–33  In 1300 Pope Boniface VIII (see especially *Inferno* 19 and
*Purgatorio* 1) proclaimed a jubilee year which brought an influx
of some 200,000 pilgrims to Rome. Dante refers to the methods
of crowd control devised at the time: central barriers were
erected on the Ponte degli Angeli to divide those pedestrians
approaching Saint Peter's from those who were leaving it – that
is, those who were heading towards the papal fortress of Castel
Sant' Angelo from those who were going in the direction of
Monte Giordano, a small hill opposite the fortress.

49f  Venedico Caccianemico (d. *c.* 1302) was a Bolognese noble of the
Guelf party and military governor of various cities. No record
remains as to how or to whom he prostituted his sister Ghisola-
bella. At line 51 the word translated as 'pickle' is '*salse*', which
as well as meaning a hot sauce may also refer to an area of Bol-
ogna in which the bodies of excommunicants and suicides were
buried.

61  'Yeah' translates Dante's '*sipa*' – Bolognese dialect for 'yes'.

85–96  The story of Jason and Hypsipyle appears in Ovid's *Metamor-
phoses* 7: 1–424, his *Heroides* 6 and also in Statius's *Thebaid* 5:
29–485. Jason, the first sea traveller voyaging in pursuit of the
Golden Fleece, becomes an important point of reference for
Dante in *Paradiso* 2: 16–18 and 33: 94–6. His appearance here
is accounted for by his acts of infidelity and seduction. When
Jason and his Argonauts arrive at the island of Lemnos, they find
that the women of the island have resolved to kill all men – but
that Hypsipyle has enabled her father, the king, to escape. The
Argonauts are accepted as husbands by the women of Lemnos.
Hypsipyle (see also *Purgatorio* 22: 112 and 26: 95) marries
Jason, only to be deserted and left pregnant when he leaves.
Medea, at line 96, after bearing two children to Jason, is out-
raged when Jason abandons her for Glauce, daughter of the king
of Corinth, and, in revenge, murders both Glauce and her own
children in the sight of Jason.

121–2  Alessio Interminei (*fl.* 1295) was a White Guelf of Lucca. For
further satirical references to Lucca, see *Inferno* 21: 37–51.

133  Thais the prostitute appears in Terence's comedy *The Eunuch*
(161 BC), but Dante would have found references to her in
Cicero's *De Amicitia* (45–44 BC) and John of Salisbury's *Poli-
craticus* (1159), where flattery is treated as a form of fraud.

# CANTO 19

*Simony exemplified by papal corruption.*
*Dante reproves Pope Nicholas III.*

**1f** The sin punished in this pocket is simony: the abuse of sacramental authority for the purposes of gain. This sin is traced to the apostolic era: in the Acts of the Apostles 8: 9–24, Simon of Samaria (the 'Magus') is condemned by Saint Peter when he seeks to buy from the Apostles the sacramental powers of their priesthood (lines 1–4). The apocryphal Acts of Saint Peter represents Simon as chief magician to Emperor Nero, defeated in miracle-working contests by Saint Peter. The punishment that Dante devises for the followers of Simon – plunged absurdly one above the other in a well, with the soles of their projecting feet set alight – involves a continuous line of corrupt pontiffs which parodies the apostolic succession.

**4–6** The trumpet call – a feature of the military epic – is translated into the prophetic instrument that will sound, once and for all, on Judgement Day. See Hosea 8 and Matthew 24: 31.

**16–21** The Baptistery in Florence contained octagonal fonts into which four pits were built, where the priest would stand to administer the sacrament of baptism. Dante makes elliptical reference to an episode when he seems to have damaged one of the fonts in the Florentine Baptistery in order to save a child from drowning. There exists no independent corroboration, but the implications are consistent with Dante's concerns in this canto: he has attempted to act as the true priest in saving life; and for doing so, his own name and reputation have been attacked by materially minded Church authorities.

**46–51** The upturned sinner is Pope Nicholas III (*c.* 1225–80), a member of the noble Orsini clan, whose family emblem was the Bear (see line 70). Under Florentine law, hired assassins were condemned to be executed by being buried head downwards in the earth.

**52–7** Boniface VIII was born into the noble clan of the Caetani in 1235, became cardinal in 1281 and pope on the resignation of Celestine V (see note to *Inferno* 3: 58–60) in 1295. In his attempts to advance the temporal ambitions of the Church he came into conflict with Philip IV (the Fair) of France over the right of the king to tax the clergy. He excommunicated Philip and issued the bull *Unam sanctam* (1302). Philip replied by declaring his election invalid and arresting Boniface at his birth-place, Anagni, in 1303. On both philosophical and perhaps personal grounds, Dante reserves a particular odium for this pope. (See especially *Inferno* 27 and *Purgatorio* 20.)

82–96  The 'lawless shepherd', the third pope, is Bernard Le Got (*c.* 1260–1314) (a Frenchman from Gascony), who became Pope Clement V. His election seems to have depended upon the influence of Philip IV (the Fair) of France. Clement immediately appointed a considerable number of French cardinals and then established the Papal Curia in Avignon, preparing for the long period in which, under French dominion, the papacy was 'exiled' from Rome. Dante is referring here not to Jason the Argonaut, who appears in *Inferno* 18, but Jason Maccabaeus, who attempted to bribe the Seleucid King Antiochus IV Epiphanes (2 Maccabees 4: 7f). Clement V is the 'new' Jason in that he may have bribed Philip into supporting his election as pope.

97–9  There is a (now discredited) story which suggests that Nicholas accepted a bribe to join the conspiracy that led to the expulsion of the Angevins from Sicily in 1282.

106–11  Saint John the Evangelist in Revelation speaks of the utter corruption which will immediately precede the Second Coming (see notes to *Inferno* 17). The Whore of Babylon is a great sign of this corruption, as at Revelation 17: 3–6:

> I saw a woman sit upon a scarlet coloured beast, full of names of blasphemy, having seven heads and seven horns. And the woman was arrayed in purple and scarlet colour, and decked with gold and precious stones and pearls, having a golden cup in her hand full of abominations and filthiness of her fornication ... And I saw the woman drunken with the blood of the saints, and with the blood of the martyrs of Jesus ...

The seven heads may be taken to represent the seven sacraments, the ten horns the Ten Commandments that were once a source of virtue and have now been polluted. Dante shares with the 'spiritual Franciscans' of his time a willingness to identify this monstrosity with the corruption of the Church. (Cf. *Purgatorio* 32–3.)

115–17  Emperor Constantine (*c.* 274–337), having been converted to Christianity (see also *Inferno* 27: 94–5 and *Paradiso* 20: 55), was thought to have donated the temporal power of the western part of the Empire to the Church. The document of donation was proved during the sixteenth century to be an eighth-century forgery. Dante had already argued that the donation was legally invalid and an offence against the spirit of Christian poverty. (See *De Monarchia* 3: 10: 1.)

# CANTO 20

*The soothsayers. Virgil's account of the founding of Mantua.*

22f Samuel Beckett meditates on the painful meaning of line 28 in his early story 'Dante and the Lobster' (1934). He also realized that 'pity' depends upon the double meaning (in Italian) of '*pietà*', which derives from a tension between the Virgilian notion of '*pietas*' as the public duty of a Roman to the gods and to the State and the Romance understanding which indicates compassion and sentiment.

Beckett must also have this episode in mind in *The Unnamable* (New York, Grove 1958), p. 279:

> If I am, I am but lightly. For I feel my tears coursing over my chest and all down my back. Ah yes I am truly bathed in tears. They gather in my beard and from there, when it can hold no more – no, no beard, no hair either, it is a great smooth ball I carry on my shoulders, featureless, but for the eyes, of which only the sockets remain.

25f Virgil speaks for most of this canto, even suggesting at lines 112–14 that Dante can remember the *Aeneid* better than he, its own author, is able to. The sinners whom Virgil introduces are soothsayers drawn mainly from the pages of classical texts. There is an implicit contrast here between his position and that of others in the classical tradition. In Dante's time, Virgil had often been regarded as a soothsayer or magician. He was thought to have journeyed to the depths of Hell at the behest of a witch. But Dante here implies a contrast between sinful soothsaying and the legitimate activities of his Virgil, who is guided by providence. Virgil was the author of the *Fourth Eclogue*, which Dante in *Purgatorio* 22 explicitly takes to be a prophecy of Christ's nativity and the coming of a new age of justice.

31–9  In Statius's *Thebaid*, the Amphiaraus episode runs to over 250
       lines, 7: 688–8: 126. Amphiaraus, one of the Seven Against Thebes,
       is an augur who has foreseen his own death in battle and yet,
       against his better judgement, is driven to participate in the war by
       his wife. His death and arrival in the underworld are described by
       Statius in characteristically spectacular and ornate style:

> Behold in a gaping chasm the ground yawns sheer and deep, and
> stars and shade feel mutual terror. The huge abyss engulfs him and
> swallows the horses as they try to leap across it . . . When on the
> sudden the prophet fell among the pallid shades and burst into the
> homes of the dead and the mysteries of the deep-sunken realm and
> affrighted ghosts with his armed corpse, all were horror struck . . .
>
> *Thebaid* 7: 816–19 and 8: 1–4

Statius (a poet whom Dante read with especial attention) appears
as an important character in the *Commedia* in *Purgatorio* 21–5.
(Cf. also Dante's references to Thebes in *Inferno* 32–3.)

40–46  Tiresias and Arruns appear respectively in Ovid's *Metamor-
       phoses* 3: 324–31 and Lucan's *Pharsalia* 1: 585–638. The Theban
       seer Tiresias is asked by Jove and Juno whether men or women
       take greater pleasure from lovemaking – Tiresias would know,
       since he has been both a man and a woman. Ovid then recounts
       how 'once with a blow of his staff Tiresias had outraged two
       huge serpents while mating; and immediately was changed from
       man to woman. Eight years later he saw the same serpents again,
       struck them once more and was changed back into a man.'
         Lucan describes Arruns as 'one who dwelt in the deserted city
       of Lucca: the course of thunderbolts, the marks on entrails yet
       warm and the warning of each wing that strays through the sky
       had no secrets from him'. Arruns foresees the disasters of civil
       war between Caesar and Pompey but conceals the whole truth.
         The references here anticipate the great description of meta-
       morphosis in *Inferno* 25, where Dante claims to outdo both
       Ovid and Lucan.

52–60  Manto is the daughter of Tiresias and herself a sorceress, who
       at the fall of Thebes – the city sacred to the god Bacchus – searched
       over many lands for a new home (as Aeneas did at the fall of
       Troy), eventually settling in the marshes around Mantua. Dante's
       (modified) account draws on Virgil's *Aeneid* 10: 198–201.

61–99  This lengthy account of the foundation of Mantua follows the
       downward course of the river Mincius, or Mincio, and attempts

to dissociate the city from any taint of sorcery. It is founded for good military and defensive reasons. The words that Dante attributes to Virgil contain topographical references to an Italian landscape that Dante himself may have travelled through, and define the place in terms of modern and Christian history. Garda is a city on the shores of Lake Benacus (the Latin name for Lake Garda). The 'central point' is, presumably, the island of Lechi, at which the dioceses of Trent, Brescia and Verona meet. Peschiera in Dante's time was controlled by the Scaligeri, lords of Verona; Govérnolo is a mile north of the point at which the Mincio meets the Po; in 1291 Pinamonte dei Bonacolsi (d. 1293) tricked the then-ruler of Mantua, Alberto de Casalodi, into withdrawing his nobles from the city. Pinamonte then stirred up the populace in rebellion and massacred most of the noble families.

106–12  Eurypylus is mentioned along with Calchas in Virgil's *Aeneid* 2: 114, which Dante seems to have misread, assuming that Eurypylus was an augur associated with Calchas in deciding when the Greek fleet should cast off for Troy from Aulis (where the oracles of Apollo were heard). In the period of the Trojan War, Greece was 'void of men', in that all its males had gone off to battle.

115–17  Michael Scott (d. *c.* 1235) was employed by Emperor Frederick II (see *Inferno* 10: 119) as a futurologist. He also translated from Arabic and from Aristotle's Greek texts.

118–20  Guido Bonatti (b. *c.* 1220) was, like Michael Scott, an astrologer at Frederick II's court and influential in Ghibelline circles. Asdente (meaning 'the Toothless') was a soothsaying shoemaker, whom Dante refers to in *Convivio* 4: 16: 6 as the most famous man in Parma.

124–30  As seen from Jerusalem, the moon is now setting south of Seville. The time is 6 a.m. The moon had been full when Dante entered the dark wood, and had cast an imperfect light that hindered rather than guided him. Dante's language briefly turns enigmatic in its references to the moon. There is a touch of the uncanny (and some archaism of language) in mentioning the folk tale of Cain as the man in the moon, carrying a bundle of thorns on his back. But the purpose of this reference is not necromantic. Rather, it is an attempt, by reference to natural phenomena, to establish a timetable for Dante's onward journey. To speak of Virgil 'chatting' here reflects Dante's use of the Florentine dialect word *introcque* (meaning 'meanwhile') which Dante in *De Vulgari Eloquentia* 1: 13: 1 declares unsuitable for poetry in the high, tragic style. This usage is the more striking in view of the mention of Virgilian 'tragedy' (line 113) and of Dantean 'comedy' in the opening verse of the following canto.

# CANTO 21

*The sinners here have been guilty of corruption in public office (barratry). The mock epic of the demon guardians of the circle.*

**7–18** The Arsenal, or shipyard, of the Venetian empire had been in existence about 200 years when Dante visited it. It developed very early a form of production-line manufacture, accurately depicted by Dante in contrast to the unproductive activity of Hell.

**37–49** Rotklors ('*Malebranche*') is an invented collective noun referring to the devils of this pocket. (Cf. '*Malacoda*', 'Evil Tail', translated at line 76 as 'Rottentail', and '*Malebolge*', 'Evil Pockets' – see note to *Inferno* 18: 1.) This sequence is punctuated by reference to the Black Guelf city of Lucca, in north-western Tuscany, which had a reputation for rampant civic corruption. Santa Zita (d. *c.* 1272) is the patron saint of Lucca. The Holy Face of Lucca is a crucifix – still on show in the city – carved in ebony (hence reference to 'black-faced gods'), supposedly by the Apostle Nicodemus. Its face is said to have been completed by a miracle while the Apostle slept. The Serchio is a river popular with bathers a few miles from Lucca.

The speaker (newly arrived in Hell) has been identified as Martino Bottaio, a political boss in Lucca, who died on the night of Good Friday 1300 – and hence at the same time as Dante's journey through Hell supposedly began. Exception from judgement is here made, ironically, on behalf of one of the most infamous of the Lucchese politicians, Bonturo Dati (d. after 1324), who, while ostensibly leader of the people's party, was driven out of the city by a popular uprising in 1313.

**94–6** Caprona, a Pisan fortress, surrendered to Florence in August 1289. Dante was probably present at the siege, as a member of the Florentine cavalry.

**112–14** Since the Passion of Christ and the Harrowing of Hell, which on Easter Saturday broke down the bridges of Rottenpockets through the aftershock of the earthquake, 1,266 years have passed to noon of Good Friday 1300, which is now 'yesterday' in the timetable of Dante's journey. If noon is five hours later than the present time, the hour is now Saturday, 7 a.m.

118–23  Some of the names given to the Malebranche may be deformations of family names from Lucca. Most are purely fantastical. A roughly literal translation of each would be as follows: *Alichino* – Harlequin; *Barbariccia* – Curly Beard; *Cagnazzo* – Nasty Dog; *Calcabrina* – Trample Frost; *Ciriatto* – Big Pig; *Draghignazzo* – Big Little Dragon; *Farfarello* – Flutterby; *Graffiacane* – Scratching Dog; *Libicocco* – (following suggestions by Robert Durling) Love Notch; *Malacoda* (lines 76 and 79) – Evil Tail; *Rubicante* – Red Face; *Scarmiglione* (line 105) – Tangled Hair.

# CANTO 22

*Corrupt officials, demon guardians*
*(and mock-heroic farce) continued.*

4–6  In a letter now lost, but recorded by the leading fifteenth-century historian Leonardo Bruni, Dante writes of his participation in the battle of Campaldino (11 June 1289) between the Florentine and Aretine Guelfs (see also *Purgatorio* 5: 93). 'Tournaments' involved group fights with hand weapons, as contrasted with jousts, which were mounted 'duels' with lances in the lists.

7–9  Medieval armies would go into battle with bells borne on great war wagons. The 'signs' are drawn from the constellations, from which appropriate auguries might be read.

43–54  Though commentators traditionally give this figure the name of Ciampolo (Jean-Paul) he is, perhaps significantly, not named in the text but simply identified by the king under which he was born, Thibaut II of Navarre (1255–70).

79–90  Between 1275 and 1296, Brother Gomita (a member of the *frati godenti* – see notes to *Inferno* 23: 103–8) acted as deputy to Nino Visconti (see *Purgatorio* 8) as governor of Gallura, one of the four administrative districts of Sardinia. Logodoro was another district, governed, it seems, by Lord Michel Zanche as deputy of King Enzo (1239?–72). At *Inferno* 33: 134, Michel Zanche is said to have been murdered by his son-in-law, Branca d'Oria.

118–20 To designate the 'sport' which Dante now describes to his readers, the poet ironically uses the elevated Latinism '*ludo*' (*ludus*). (Cf. his address to the reader at *Inferno* 16: 127–8.)

# CANTO 23

*The conclusion of Dante's encounter with the devils.*
*The hypocrites. Caiaphas.*

4–6 Aesop's *Fables* circulated widely in the late Middle Ages. In the fable to which Dante refers here, a frog offers to transport a mouse across the water and ties its leg to his, meaning to dive and drown it. As frog and mouse struggle together, a hawk descends and carries off both of them.

7–9 The Italian words used here, '*mo*' and '*issa*', both mean 'now' or 'soon' – '*issa*' being a form used in the dialect of Lucca.

61–3 Cluny was the Benedictine monastery in Burgundy, founded in 910, which by the twelfth century possessed the largest church in Christendom – but also a growing reputation for easy living.

64–6 Emperor Frederick II (see *Inferno* 10) punished traitors by encasing them in leaden cloaks, then melting these encasements around them, over a slow fire.

103–8 '*Frati godenti*' (here translated as 'good-time friars') was the disparaging nickname given to the religious order of the Knights of Saint Mary, founded in Bologna in 1261, which allegedly devoted itself to civic peace but was notorious for corruption. Two of its founding members – Catalano dei Malavolti (1210–85) and Loderingo degli Andalo (1210–93), the first a Guelf, the second a Ghibelline – were appointed to the governorship of Florence in 1266 by Pope Clement IV (d. 1268), ostensibly to maintain a troubled peace. Dante clearly suspected their motive. It was they who ordered the demolition of many Ghibelline houses in the Gardingo ('Watchtower') district of Florence, close to the present Palazzo della Signoria, including the dwelling of Farinata degli Uberti. (See *Inferno* 10 and Villani's *Cronica* 7: 13.)

115–23 Caiaphas, the High Priest of Jerusalem (son-in-law of Annas (line 121)), judges Christ and declares that it is expedient that 'one man should die for the people' (John 11: 45–52), thus ignoring the redemptive significance of Christ in favour of a partial, pragmatic judgement.

# CANTO 24

*Climbing from the pocket of the hypocrites, Dante
and Virgil arrive at a point where they can look down
into the pocket of the thieves.*

1–3 Aquarius (the zodiacal sign of the Waterbearer) is in the ascend-
ant between 21 January and 21 February. Thus the winter
solstice has passed and night has begun to come closer in length
to day – or else, in some interpretations, 'runs southwards'.

49–51 Virgil's heroic exhortation may owe something to *Aeneid*
5: 740.

55–7 For the geography of Purgatory (conceived as a mountain in the
southern hemisphere), see note to *Inferno* 34: 103–33.

91–3 The heliotrope is a stone that was believed, in medieval studies
of the properties of minerals, to render its possessor invisible.

106–11 Dante's description of the phoenix draws directly on Ovid's
*Metamorphoses* 15: 392–407. But it is also a familiar medieval
figure for the Resurrection – in which, according to Christian
belief, human beings are finally assured of the eternal possession
of their own physical identities.

121–6 Vanni Fucci was a member of the White Guelf faction in Pis-
toia. He was responsible for the murder of a fellow White Guelf
in 1293 or 1294. In 1293 (lines 137–8), he stole two silver tab-
lets bearing images of the Blessed Virgin and the Apostles from
the sacristy of the church of San Zeno at Pistoia. Rampino di
Francesco Foresi was arrested for the crime and only released in
1295, when Vanni Fucci informed on one of his accomplices
(line 139), who was subsequently executed in Rampino's place.

142–51 This violent and perhaps deliberately enigmatic prophecy
pictures the factional conflicts of the Tuscan Blacks and Whites
in terms of the geography of the region. Mars, the god of war,
stirs up the leader of the Blacks of Lucca, Moroello Malaspina,
from his native place in the Val di Magra. (For Dante's eulogy of
the Malaspina family, see *Purgatorio* 8.) The 'clouds' (line 146)
are probably the Tuscan White Guelfs. Conflicts flared in 1302
and in 1306, when, in alliance with the Blacks of Florence,
Moroello defeated the Whites of Pistoia.

# CANTO 25

*The thieves continued, their punishment to be
constantly metamorphosed from human form to
reptile and back again.*

1–3 The obscene sign of the figs is made by thrusting the thumb
between the two forefingers. The Florentine chronicler Villani
reports (*Cronica* 6: 5) that in 1228 Pistoia set up a marble repre-
sentation of the figs aimed at Florence. The name Pistoia is derived,
says Villani (*Cronica* 1: 32), from the Latin '*pestis*' ('pestilence').

10–12 These lines represent the first of a series of polemical outbursts
against the cities of Tuscany, including Florence itself (cf. *Inferno*
26 and 33, and also the satire against Siena that concludes
*Inferno* 29). In his authorial voice, Dante enters vigorously into
the political animosities of the period.

13–18 Dante here employs the elevated and Latinate locution
'*verbo*' – which he also uses in referring to the 'Word of God' or
*Logos*. The rhyme '*verbo*' ('word') and '*acerbo*' (here, 'sour')
also occurs in the account of Satan's fall in *Paradiso* 19. It is a
further sign of the literary self-consciousness that characterizes
this canto that Dante should introduce two cross-references to
earlier passages in his own fiction: Capaneus (who was 'flung
down from Theban walls' (line 15)) appears at *Inferno* 14: 49–75;
the centaurs from whom Cacus is separated are guardians of the
circle of Hell described in *Inferno* 12.

25–33 Virgil recounts the outline of the story of Cacus as he himself
had told it in *Aeneid* 8: 193f. Dante has greatly transformed
the Virgilian account, in which Cacus appears not as a centaur
but simply as a monstrous half-man, who steals the cattle of
Hercules and butchers them on the Aventine Hill in Rome.

43f Though little is known about the historical lives of the five figures
who participate in these metamorphoses, all were Florentines.
The first two to appear may have been Agnello, of the prominent
Brunelleschi family, and Buoso Donati, who is referred to again
in *Inferno* 30. Cianfa (who is, presumably, the lizard that
responds to the question posed by Agnello and Buoso) was
another member of the important Donati clan. For the last two
men, see note to lines 148–51.

94–9 For Lucan's *Pharsalia* – an account of the Roman civil wars fought in the deserts of Libya – see notes to *Inferno* 20. In Ovid's *Metamorphoses* 6: 571–603, Cadmus, founder of Thebes, is transformed into a serpent as a punishment for impiety, along with his wife Harmonia. Arethusa, in *Metamorphoses* 5: 572–641, is transformed into a stream while escaping the advances of Alpheus – who is himself transformed into a stream and so mingles with her.

136–8 Human spittle was thought in Dante's day to be venomous to snakes.

148–51 The last two Florentines are probably Puccio Galigai, who was nicknamed '*Sciancato*' ('the Lame') and Francesco de' Cavalcanti – originally the 'snakelet' of line 84 – whose nickname was '*Guercio*' ('Cross-eyed'). Francesco was murdered by the inhabitants of the village of Gaville, on whom the Cavalcanti clan took extreme vengeance. In that sense Gaville weeps on his account.


# CANTO 26

*The first of two cantos describing the eighth pocket,*
*where the sinners, transformed into flames, are those*
*who have made deceitful or destructive use of their*
*intellectual gifts.*


1–3 Behind this sarcastic encomium one may discern the words inscribed in 1255 on the walls of the Bargello Palace in Florence claiming for the republic (ironically enough) imperial dominion over the world and the right to make its Tuscan subjects 'happy': '*Que mare, que terram, que totum possidet orbem*' ('Who possesses land, sea and all the earthly globe'; a phrase from Lucan's *Pharsalia* 1: 109, describing the self-destructiveness of Rome, also quoted in Dante's *De Monarchia* 2: 8). A connection is clearly drawn between intellectual appetitiveness and commercial greed. (See *Convivio* 4: 12: 11.)

7–9 As with the reference to Pistoia in *Inferno* 25, this allusion points to the strife, particularly between Black and White Guelf factions, that had arisen in the last decade of the thirteenth century between Florence and the Tuscan cities, such as Prato, that were its immediate neighbours.

**34–9** These lines refer, in highly compressed form, to the two Old Testament prophets Elijah and Elisha, contained in 2 Kings 2. Elijah is, like Ulysses, hidden in flame, but ascends to Heaven (as, of course, Ulysses does not):

> And it came to pass, as they still went on, and talked, that, behold, there appeared a chariot of fire, and horses of fire, and parted them both asunder; and Elijah went up by a whirlwind into heaven.
>
> And Elisha saw it, and he cried, My father, my father, the chariot of Israel, and the horsemen thereof.
>
> 2 Kings 2: 11–12

Elisha is 'avenged by furious bears' for being mocked by the urchins of Bethel:

> there came forth little children out of the city, and mocked him, and said unto him, Go up, thou bald head; go up, thou bald head . . . And there came forth two she bears out of the wood, and tare forty and two children of them.
>
> 2 Kings 2: 23–4

**46–8** The destructive fire within is now displayed in the outward fire that consumes the sinners.

**52–63** Statius describes how the two sons of Oedipus, Eteocles and Polynices, kill each other in mutual hatred and are laid on the same funeral pyre, their hatred dividing its fire (*Thebaid* 12: 429–32). Drawing on a number of classical sources, including Virgil's *Aeneid* 2 and Ovid's *Metamorphoses* 13: 123–380, Dante puts into Virgil's mouth references to three events in Ulysses's life, all of which might be taken as evidence of a destructive or impious intellect worthy of damnation. First, Ulysses devises the stratagem of the Trojan horse, which allows the Greeks to enter Troy and destroy it – thus opening the way to the ultimate foundation of Rome. (Both Ulysses and Diomed entered Troy in the wooden belly of the horse.) Secondly, Ulysses persuades Achilles (in Statius's *Achilleid* 1) to abandon his love for his wife Deidamia, daughter of the king of Scyros, and go off to the Trojan War, in which he meets his death. Thirdly, in both the *Aeneid* and the *Metamorphoses*, Ulysses is held to have been guilty of profanity, when he stealthily enters Troy and steals from its inner sanctum the sacred image of Pallas Athene (the Palladium) on which the security of the city depends. (See also note to lines 85f.)

73–84 The rhetorical devices that Dante attributes to Virgil reflect features of Virgil's own usage in, for instance, *Aeneid* 4: 317–18.

85f Continuing the challenge to classical literature that he issued in *Inferno* 25, Dante undertakes to represent the figure of the famously intelligent Ulysses. He did not know Homer's Greek original, and so relied on references in Latin sources, including Cicero, Seneca and, above all, Horace's *Ars Poetica* and Ovid's *Metamorphoses* 14: 157. But these sources all tend to represent Ulysses in terms of low cunning rather than intelligence – as does Virgil in lines 55–63 of this canto. Nor has any precedent been found that anticipates the account which Dante puts in Ulysses's own mouth of a last journey beyond the limits imposed by the gods upon human endeavour (lines 108–9), a journey which ends in death but is impelled by a desire for knowledge of the world and of the vices and virtues of human beings (lines 98–9 and 116–20). In subsequent cantos of the *Commedia*, Dante makes more frequent mention of, or allusion to, the Ulysses story than any other episode in the poem. (See *Purgatorio* 1: 131 and 19: 22–4; *Paradiso* 2: 1–6 and 27: 82–4.)

91–9 The sorceress Circe, daughter of the sun, demanded that Ulysses – on his adventurous return from the Trojan War – should remain with her on the island of Aeaea, near Cumae, for a full year after she has transformed his men from swine back to human form. (See Ovid, *Metamorphoses* 14.) Aeneas on his more purposeful and 'pious' journey renames a promontory in the vicinity Gaeta, in honour of his nurse who died there. (See also Virgil, *Aeneid* 7: 1–4, 97–9.) In attributing to Ulysses this burning intellectual curiosity, Dante draws directly on phrasing in Horace's *Ars Poetica* 141–42, which in turn refers to the opening lines of Homer's *Odyssey*.

100–42 The geography of this invented journey represents Ulysses as travelling through the Mediterranean – seeing both its northern and southern shores and the island of Sardinia – and then passing through the Straits of Gibraltar (the rocks of which were supposed, since Pindar's *Fourth Nemean Ode*, to have been set up by Hercules as a limit on human travel), leaving Seville on the right and Ceuta in Morocco on the left. Turning south – and therefore left – Ulysses journeys for five months, telling time by the phases of the moon; and as he enters the southern hemisphere, he sees the stars around the northern pole disappear as those stars of the southern hemisphere (never before seen by human eyes since the fall of Adam – see *Purgatorio* 1: 22–4) gradually appear to view. The mountain that Ulysses encounters is Mount Purgatory. This is, in Dante's view, the only land mass in the southern hemisphere. It stands at the antipodes of Jerusalem and its formation is described in the final canto of the *Inferno*.

## CANTO 27

*Abuse of intellect continued; the case of*
*Guido da Montefeltro.*

7–12 Phalarus, the despot of Acragas in Sicily, had a bronze bull made by Perillus of Athens. Within the bronze bull, the tyrant's victims would be roasted alive; a mechanical larynx translated the roars of the victim roasted within its hollow body into the bellowing of a bull. The first victim was the artificer himself. The passage in the Italian is syntactically disturbed and marked by unusual repetitions. But the essential message is clear: 'the biter bit', a villain hoist with his own petard.

19f The damned soul is not, as Ulysses was, a legendary pagan but a historical figure from the Christian era who enjoyed a close working relationship with the pope – the Ghibelline warlord and politician Guido da Montefeltro (1223–98). There had been a time when Dante admired Guido. In the *Convivio* 4: 28: 8, he spoke of him as 'the most noble Guido of Montefeltro', and praised him for the wisdom he displayed at the end of his life. Guido, after a history of excommunications, finally reconciled himself with the Church, and, having associated himself with the Franciscans, died in Assisi. In this early work, then, Guido is taken to exemplify an important point in Dantean ethics that human life goes through four phases and each has its characteristic virtues, which the intellect should seek to cultivate to the full. For instance, in what we should now call middle age and Dante calls youth – or '*gioventute*' – we should usefully be involved in practical and public affairs (since etymologically the word '*gioventute*' can be derived from '*giovare*' – 'to be useful'). Both Ulysses and Guido continue to behave as though they were, in this sense, youthful and useful. Yet both were old men at the time of their deaths, and by that time should have begun to develop the virtues of contemplation, considering the life-to-come.

Lines 19–21 may be taken as a sign of Guido's political divisiveness (see note to lines 28–54) in that, far from recognizing in Virgil a representative of true imperial authority, he focuses, perhaps disparagingly, on Virgil's Lombard accent and turn of phrase: '*Istra*' ('now') being used in the Italian text instead of the word '*issa*' which might have been expected here. (Note that Virgil at line 33 may respond by allowing Dante to speak to this mere Italian in the vernacular.)

28–54  Where most of the cities of Italy in the last decades of the thirteenth century had come under Guelf control, the Romagna, in the north-east, had remained Ghibelline in sympathy, largely through the military and strategic efforts of Guido, who locates his birthplace at lines 29–30 between Urbino (where he became duke in 1293) and the source of the Tiber. But Ghibelline control had begun to slip, leaving in its wake Guelf despotisms. In response to Guido's question, Dante ascribes to himself a survey of the political state of the seven major cities of the Romagna. Notably, they are described as despotisms (line 37), suggesting – against the claims of true empire – the assumption of violent and unlawful rule. Despots, as Aristotle (quoted in *De Monarchia* 3: 4) declares, 'do not follow laws for the common good but attempt to wrench them to their own benefit'. Dante then proceeds to describe these cities in terms, usually, of the heraldic emblems and coats-of-arms of their leading families. Since 1275 Ravenna had been ruled by the Guelf Guido Vecchio da Polenta (father of Francesca, who appears in *Inferno* 5) and in 1283 Guido da Montefeltro lost control of the town of Cervia to the Polenta, whose family emblem was a red eagle on a golden field. Forlì had been defended successfully by Guido against troops dispatched by Pope Martin IV. These troops included French mercenaries whom Guido massacred, leaving a 'bloodstained pile' (line 44) of the dead. In 1296, however, the city came under the control of the Guelf Ordelaffi. Their shield bore a green lion with prominent claws in its upper half. Rimini was ruled by the Malatesta, whose ancient stronghold was Verucchio and whose emblem was the bull mastiff – its teeth sucking the life blood out of its opponents. Ferocious adversaries of Guido, the Malatesta had driven the Ghibellines from Rimini in 1295 and imprisoned and murdered their leader, Montagna de' Parcitati, in 1296. Faenza and Imola are identified by the rivers that flow through them, the Lamone and the Santerno. These cities were ruled by the Pagani family, under the emblem of a blue lion on a white field. Maghinardo Pagani (d. 1302) fought as a Ghibelline in Romagna, north of the Apennines, and as a Guelf to the south, in Tuscany. The last of the seven is Cesena on the river Savio, which was governed nominally by Guido's nephew Galasso, but in 1300 was a Guelf commune, living politically – as it did topographically – between the high mountains of tyranny and the plains of republican democracy.

85–97  The 'lord of our new Pharisees' is Pope Boniface VIII (see notes to *Inferno* 19). He had called on Guido for advice in prosecuting his quarrel with the Colonna clan of Rome, who refused to admit the legitimacy of his election in 1294. The Colonna had retreated to their fortress at Penestrina (or Palestrina, formerly Praeneste), twenty miles east of Rome. Boniface's campaign against this citadel is contrasted with what Dante might have considered more legitimate objects of military action, particularly the recovery of Acre in the Holy Land, which had been seized by Muslim forces in 1291. Further ironies in the corrupting complicity of Church and State are identified by the parallel drawn between the emperor Constantine (see notes to *Inferno* 19) and Pope Sylvester I (314–35) and Boniface himself and Guido. The legend is that Constantine was stricken by leprosy for his persecution of the Christians, was cured on Mount Soracte, north of Rome, by Sylvester and subsequently converted to Christianity. Boniface's disease is not leprosy but a frenzied political ambition. The 'cure' is not a conversion but the involvement in an intrigue and abuse of absolution that leads Guido to Hell.

112–23  The devil identifies the false logic that runs through lines 101–11: that absolution cannot be given in advance of the crime that it is intended to pardon. Willing a sin and not willing it cannot, logically, be simultaneous. In *Purgatorio* 5, a scene occurs that exactly parallels the farcical tussle over Guido's soul at the gate of Heaven. But in this case, Guido's son, Buonconte da Montefeltro (d. 1289), receives unexpectedly the salvation which his father, for all *his* expectations, is firmly denied. Buonconte was no contemplative. He was a warrior who died in battle, fighting on the opposite side from Dante. Yet Buonconte's final act on earth is pictured as an infinitesimally small moment of repentance in which he weeps a penitent tear and locks his arms over his chest in the form of a cross.

# CANTO 28

*The ninth pocket, where those whose words have*
*deliberately fomented discord between others are*
*punished by the suffering of wounds.*

1–21 '[S]et loose' ('*sciolte*') in line 1 points to a distinction between
tightly disciplined verse and the laxer form of prose, as used by
historians such as Livy. Apulia in Dante's day was the whole of
southern Italy, forming the kingdom of Naples. The following
lines make rapid but detailed reference to the wars that were
fought in this territory from ancient times up to the present.
These include the battles fought between the Trojans (that is to
say, the original Romans) and the native Latin tribes. The 'long
war where rings were heaped' (line 12) refers to the Punic Wars
of 264–146 BC, fought between Rome and Carthage for domin-
ion over the Mediterranean, as recounted by Livy; it is reported
by Saint Augustine of Hippo and Paulus Orosius that, following
the battle of Cannae (216 BC), the Carthaginians gathered three
bushels of rings as spoils from the Roman dead. Robert Guiscard
(*c.* 1015–85) was the first of a line of Norman rulers of Sicily and
southern Italy invited to stake a claim to these territories by Pope
Nicholas II (d. 1061) in 1059. Southern domination of Italy was
extinguished with the death of Emperor Frederick II's natural
son, Manfred, at the battle of Benevento in 1266. (See *Purgato-
rio* 3.) On Dante's understanding, the battle was lost when
Apulian barons deserted their positions near the Ceperano pass.
At Tagliacozzo, in the Abruzzi hills north-east of Rome, the last
remaining hopes of the imperial cause were extinguished in 1268
with the defeat of Coradino, Frederick's grandson, by Charles of
Anjou (1227–85), following tactical advice from 'Alardo' (Érard
de Valéry, Constable of Champagne (*c.* 1220–77)).

31–3 The Prophet Mohammed (*c.* 570–632) was thought to have
been a Nestorian Christian before arriving at his own religious
vision. He may thus be judged a schismatic. Ali (*c.* 600–661) was
Mohammed's cousin and son-in-law.

55–60 These lines refer to the agitated religious scene – evoked pow-
erfully by Umberto Eco in *The Name of the Rose* (1980) – which
developed in Italy around 1300. Dolcino de' Tornielli (in some
measure similar to Dante in his radical view of social order) was

leader of the band of Apostolic Brothers and preached that pos-
sessions should be held in common. Pope Clement V moved
against him 1305, with soldiers drawn from Dolcino's native
Novara. Dolcino was captured and burned at the stake in 1307.

73–5 Though little is known about Pier da Medicina, early commen-
tators suggest that he was responsible for sowing strife among
the members of the Polenta and Malatesta families in the 1280s.
(See notes to *Inferno* 27.)

76–90 Guido del Cassero and Angiolello da Carignano, leading
figures in the city of Fano, were drowned between 1312 and
1317 (with stones slung around their necks) off the coast of
Cattolica, near Rimini, on the orders of Malatestino, the des-
potic lord of Rimini. The currents and winds were particularly
dangerous on this coastline. But since these two men were
doomed to be murdered, there was no point in their praying for
safe passage.

94–102 Gaius Scribonius Curio (d. 49 BC) first advised Caesar to
cross the river Rubicon near Rimini, thus precipitating the
Roman civil wars.

106–8 Mosca de' Lamberti (*fl.* 1200), a Florentine, first mentioned by
Ciacco in *Inferno* 6, is thought to have stirred up the strife that
ran through the families of Florence throughout the thirteenth
century. When Buondelmonte de' Buondelmonti (*fl.* 1200) re-
jected the wife from the Amidei clan to whom he was betrothed,
Mosca – whose Lamberti family were allied to the Amidei –
incited his allies to revenge with the words: 'What's done, well,
that is done.' On Easter Sunday 1215, Buondelmonte was
dragged from his horse and stabbed to death.

133f The final figure is the troubadour poet Bertran de Born (*c.* 1140–
*c.* 1215), lord of the castle of Altaforte in Périgord. Famously, the
poetry of Bertran displays a positive relish in the destructive ener-
gies released by warfare and battle, as for instance in his '*Be·m
plai lo gais temps de pascor*' with its great, ironic crescendo of
blood lust:

> How pleased I am with the season of Easter, which makes leaves and
> flowers flourish. And I am pleased when I hear birds in all happiness
> send their song ringing through the woodland. And I am pleased
> when across the fields I see tents and pavilions pitched and am greatly
> cheered when I see lined up on the plain the ranks of horsemen and
> horses. And I am pleased when the skirmishers put crowd and all

their possessions to flight, and cheered when after them I see a great
host of men in arms come in pursuit.

In *De Vulgari Eloquentia* 2: 2: 8, Dante speaks highly of Ber-
tran. Lamenting that the Italian vernacular has yet to provide an
example of military poetry, he points to Bertran's poetry as an
exemplar of what the Occitan vernacular has already achieved.
Now, however, this surreal picture of the brilliant Bertran carry-
ing his own severed head like a lantern markedly modifies the
earlier celebration. If Bertran is in Hell, it is because – in a spirit
of political realism – his interference in the affairs of the English
court has led to acrimony between father and son. An exact cor-
respondence of crime and punishment is observed.

Dante puts in Bertran's mouth, in the final line of this canto,
the one use of the word '*contrapasso*' ('counter-suffering'), which
is sometimes taken to characterize the whole vengeance system
of the *Inferno*. One way in which Dante may be thought to have
moved on is in his realization that only God's apparent ven-
geance is a guarantee of wholeness.

136–8 In 2 Samuel 15–19, Ahithophel, the friend and adviser to King
David, incites David's son Absalom to rebel against his father.


# CANTO 29

*Conclusion to the ninth pocket. Entry into the tenth
and last pocket, where deceit in the form of false
science, counterfeiting and impersonation is punished.*

10–12 This establishes the time as about 1 p.m. on Holy Saturday.
Dante must hurry on if he is to arrive at Purgatory by Easter Sun-
day morning.

19–21 This is Geri del Bello (lines 25–7), the first cousin of Dante's
father, who was murdered by the Sachetti clan around 1280 and
(according to the commentary on the *Commedia* written by
Dante's son Pietro) eventually requited in 1310.

46–51 The Valdichiana and Maremma areas in Tuscany were, along
with Sardinia, notorious for malaria in Dante's day.

58–65 Ovid tells in *Metamorphoses* 7: 523–660 how the people of
Aegina (an island off the coast of Athens) were struck by a
plague visited on them by Juno. Aeacus, king of Aegina, prayed

for help to Jupiter and in a dream saw ants becoming men. The
new inhabitants of the island, the Myrmidons, were transformed
into human form from the ants that lived in an oak sacred to
Jupiter. (See also *Convivio* 4: 37: 17.)

109–20  This speaker is the alchemist Griffolino of Arezzo, executed in
1272, whose claim to be able to fly like Daedalus was taken ser-
iously by a Sienese nobleman, Alberto of Siena, who was greatly
favoured by, and possibly the son of, the bishop inquisitor of
Siena. When Griffolino failed to perform the promised miracle,
Alberto persuaded the bishop to have him burned at the stake.

124–39  Continuing his satirical attack on Sienese folly, Dante – through
the mouth of Capocchio, who is said in one early commentary to
have been a student friend of Dante's in Florence – names a group
of prominent figures who formed the '*Brigata Spendereccia*'
('Spendthrifts Club'). Of these it has been possible to identify Cac-
cia d'Asciano (d. after 1293) and Bartolommeo dei Folcacchieri
(d. 1300), also known as '*l'Abbagliato*' ('Dazzledeye'), who held
important posts in the Guelf administration of Tuscany, and Cac-
cianemico degli Scialenghi d'Asciano. The unidentified 'Nick' (line
127) seems to have dabbled in the expensive trade of spice cloves.
Capocchio himself, according to contemporary anecdotes, was
discovered, one Good Friday, painting the whole story of Christ's
Passion on his fingernails. Dante caught him in the act and, when
Capocchio hurriedly erased these images, berated him for having
destroyed such a wonderful work of art. Capocchio was burned at
the stake as an alchemist in Siena in 1293.

# CANTO 30

*Falsifiers continued: Master Adam, the counterfeiter;*
*quarrels between Adam and Sinon, Virgil and Dante.*

1–21  In Ovid's *Metamorphoses* 4: 465–542, Juno is stirred to jeal-
ousy by Jove's adultery with Semele, daughter of Cadmus,
founder of Thebes. She takes revenge by driving Athamas (hus-
band of Ino, another daughter of Cadmus) to bring about the
deaths of both his wife and sons in a fit of madness. (For Semele,
see *Paradiso* 21: 6.) Hecuba, queen of Troy at the fall of the city,
sees her daughter Polyxena sacrificed on the tomb of Achilles and
then finds the mutilated body of her son Polydorus, murdered by

King Polymnestor, thrown up on the seashore. Driven mad, she barks like a dog and kills Polymnestor by thrusting her fingers into his eyes. (See Ovid, *Metamorphoses* 13: 408–575.)

31–45 Gianni Schicchi (d. before 1280), a Florentine noble famous for his arts of mimicry, was persuaded to imitate a dying man, climbing into his deathbed to dictate a last will and testament in favour of Simone Donati (father of Forese: see *Purgatorio* 23 and Piccarda in *Paradiso* 3). In fact, Gianni employed the occasion to utter a will in his own favour, 'bequeathing' to himself the best mare in the dead man's stable. The dead man, Buoso Donati, appears as a serpent in *Inferno* 25. (See note to *Inferno* 25: 43f.) Myrrha is the legendary mother of Adonis, and in Ovid's *Metamorphoses* 10: 298–513 is said to adopt a disguise in order to seduce her own father, King Cinyras of Cyprus.

73–90 The gold florin of Florence carried on one side the lily, emblem of the city, and on the other the mark of Saint John the Baptist, its patron saint. By adding three carats of dross, Adam reduces the florin from its official twenty-four carats to twenty-one. The Branda Spring has not been securely identified. It may refer to the well of that name in Siena or another in the Casentino.

97–9 Sinon and Potiphar's wife are both guilty of false testimony. Sinon persuaded the Trojans to accept the gift of the Trojan horse. Potiphar's wife, in Genesis 39: 7–21, accused Joseph of rape when he rejected her advances.

127–9 The 'mirror' into which Narcissus looked (Ovid, *Metamorphoses* 3: 370–503) is the water in which he drowned. (See also *Paradiso* 3: 17–18.)

# CANTO 31

*The giants Nimrod, Ephialtes and Antaeus. Antaeus lowers Dante into the last region of Hell.*

4–6 An epic reference dominates the opening of this canto, comparing Virgil's words in the moment of friction that ended *Inferno* 30 to the spear that Achilles inherited from his father which alone could heal the wounds it caused. (See Ovid, *Art of Love* 4: 43–8.)

16–18 Dante recalls the disaster, described in the eleventh-century French epic poem *Chanson de Roland*, that overcame the troops of Charlemagne in 778 at the battle of Roncesvalles in the Pyr-

enees, supposedly against the forces of Muslim invaders. Betrayed
into an ambush by Ganelon, Roland, leader of Charlemagne's
rearguard, blew his horn until his brains spilt out, but to no avail.
The flower of Charlemagne's 'sacred band' (line 17) received no
help. (See especially *La Chanson de Roland*, lines 1765f.)

**40–43** Montereggione was a fortress with fourteen towers rising
above its circular curtain wall, eight miles north-west of Siena,
built as a defence by the Sienese after their victory over Florence
at Montaperti in 1260.

**58f** Nimrod was the builder of the Tower of Babel and, as such, has
been in Dante's mind since *De Vulgari Eloquentia* 1: 7, in which
false pride, in merely material domination, is associated with the
confusion of tongues and the creation of vernacular languages.
The canto confirms this emphasis, attributing to Nimrod the
nonsense that he speaks at line 67. (Cf. Plutus in *Inferno* 7.)

The bronze pine cone (line 59), some four metres high and
cast in antiquity, is now to be seen in the Vatican.

**61–6** Here (at a point when he is shortly to register the nonsense lan-
guage of Nimrod) Dante employs the word '*perizoma*', which in
the sacred tongue of Hebrew is used to refer to the apron or fig
leaf with which the first humans modestly covered themselves.
From folklore and encyclopedias, Dante gained the impression
that the northern Frisians were especially tall.

**94–124** The giants named in this sequence are: Ephialtes, son of Nep-
tune, who was sent by his father to pile up the mountains of
Ossa and Pelion (in Macedonia) so as to reach Mount Olympus
and challenge the gods, and is noted for his ferocity (Virgil,
*Aeneid* 6: 583–4); Briareus, who is spoken of here as being noth-
ing special – similar to Ephialtes – contrary to Virgil's account of
him in *Aeneid* 10: 564 (see also Statius, *Thebaid* 2: 596);
Antaeus, who does not speak, though he is able to do so, did not
attack the gods, and so is not bound, but did, however, ruin
crops and attack men and cattle in the vale of Zama in northern
Africa, until Hercules arrived to conquer him by lifting him clear
of contact with his mother – the earth – from whom he drew his
strength (see Lucan, *Pharsalia* 4: 593–660; it was in the vale of
Zama that the Roman general Scipio defeated Hannibal (lines
115–17) and ended the Carthaginian attempt to dominate the
Mediterranean); Tityos, who attempted to rape Latona, the
mother of Apollo and Diana (see Servius on *Aeneid* 6: 595), and
in punishment was stretched out over the earth, his body cover-
ing nine acres, as a vulture fed on his liver (*Aeneid* 6: 595–7);

Typhon, who was struck by a thunderbolt sent from Jupiter and buried under Mount Etna (Ovid, *Metamorphoses* 4: 303 and 5: 354f; cf. *Paradiso* 8: 68–9).

136–41 Antaeus is compared to the Garisenda tower in Bologna (still standing), which looks as though it is about to fall when a cloud passes behind it.

# CANTO 32

*The first two subdivisions of treachery, Caina*
*(treachery against kin) and Antenora (treachery*
*against party or state). The Ninth Circle of Hell.*

1–6 The opening lines develop a thought from Cicero's *Somnium Scipionis* 4: 9, which speaks of the distribution of the planetary spheres: 'The earth is the lowest sphere and does not move. So it bears the weight of all the other heavens.' Following this logic, Dante sees the centre of the earth as the point at which all weight is concentrated.

10–12 The city of Thebes (for Dante, the image of violence and corruption; see *Inferno* 33: 88–90) was built by the poet Amphion, whose verses, aided by the Muses, caused the rocks to move and become the city walls (Statius, *Achilleid* 1: 13).

13–15 The exotic reference to '*zebe*' – 'goats' or, more exotically still, 'bezoars' – recalls the Scriptural separation of sheep and goats at Judgement Day. (See Matthew 25: 32.) In the Italian the whole of the opening passage, lines 1–15, is marked by an unusual complication of style, in its rhyming and wide range of diction.

28–30 Tambernic and Pietrapana (now called Tambura and Pania della Croce) are mountain peaks in the Apuan Alps, near Lucca.

40–57 The two figures here are the brothers Alessandro and Napoleone degli Alberti, who killed each other around 1282 in a quarrel over inheritance. The Conti Alberti, including their father Alberto, owned lands and castles – Vernia and Cerbaia – in the valley of the Bisenzio, which flows into the Arno at Signa, some ten miles downriver from Florence.

58–60 Caina, the setting of the present episode, is the region of the lowest circle of Hell reserved for those who treacherously murder their kin.

**61–9** In the French prose work *Mort le roi Artu* (*c.* 1237), King Arthur kills Mordred (officially his nephew; actually his illegitimate son by Morgan le Fay). The other figures are historical, all belonging to the last decades of the thirteenth century. Focaccia is Vanni de' Cancellieri of Pistoia, who is said variously to have murdered his cousin or possibly his uncle in a tailor's shop, and to have been responsible for the division of the Guelfs into the Black and White factions (see *Inferno* 24: 142). Sassolo Mascheroni, probably of the Florentine Toschi clan, murdered his cousin for an inheritance and was beheaded after being rolled through Florence in a barrel of nails. Alberto (or Uberto) Camiscione de' Pazzi, from the Val d'Arno, killed his kinsman Ubertino for his castles. But his crime is outweighed (hence 'He'll acquit me here' (line 69)) by another of the Pazzi (the name means 'the Mad') who more grievously betrayed a fortress of the White Guelf faction for money during the campaign of the White exiles in 1302.

**70–123** At this point Dante passes from Caina into Antenora, where those who betray their country are punished. The penultimate sinner at line 122 is the archetypal traitor Ganelon, who in *La Chanson de Roland* (see notes on *Inferno* 31: 16–18) betrayed his stepson Roland into the hands of the Saracen king Marsilio at the massacre of Roncesvalles. Among the contemporary traitors is the major protagonist of this phase of the canto, Bocca degli Alberti ('Big Mouth' (line 106)), who, as a Ghibelline treacherously assuming the role of a Guelf, showed his true colours at the battle of Montaperti in 1260 (see *Inferno* 10), when he conspired in the defeat of the Guelfs by cutting the Florentine standard from the hand of its bearer. Hence the reference to 'revenge for Montaperti' (lines 80–81). Buoso da Dovero (Duera) was a Ghibelline leader of Cremona who was bribed (line 115) to allow the armies of Charles of Anjou to pass through his territory in a campaign against the imperial representative, Manfred (see *Purgatorio* 3). Tesauro dei Beccheria, abbot of Vallombrosa and papal legate in Tuscany (lines 119–20), was beheaded in 1258 for treachery towards the Guelfs. Gianni de' Soldanier ('Ghibelline Jack' (line 121)) became a Guelf after the defeat of Manfred in 1266 in his attempt to secure power. Tebaldello, a member of the Ghibelline Zambrasi clan of Faenza (line 122), opened the gates of Faenza on the morning of 13 November 1280 to allow in the enemies of a certain family – the Bolognese

Lambertazzi, who had taken refuge there – against whom he bore a grudge.

**124–39** This episode will dominate the first phase of *Inferno* 33. The reference to Tydeus and Menalippus at lines 130–32 draws on Statius's *Thebaid* 7: 745–64, where the hero Tydeus, who is dying by a wound from Menalippus's spear, asks that the severed head of Menalippus, whom he himself has slain, should be brought to him. Spurred on by the Furies, he sets his teeth into the skull, just at the moment when the goddess Minerva is about to honour his victory with a laurel crown.

# CANTO 33

*Antenora continued. Ugolino. The passage to*
*Ptolomea. Treachery against guests.*

**13f** Count Ugolino (?1230–89) was descended from an ancient Longobard Ghibelline family with possessions in the region of Pisa. He had been the imperial representative in Sardinia but, with the fall of the Hohenstaufen dynasty, he returned to Pisa and, changing his allegiances, joined the Guelf party, in the hope of gaining control of the city. While military governor of the city, he gave up certain Pisan fortresses (see lines 85–6) to the Guelf cities of Lucca and Florence, meaning to weaken the antagonism to Pisa which these cities displayed in alliance with Genova. When the Ghibelline party, under Archbishop Ruggieri degli Ubaldini (who is now Ugolino's victim in Hell), came once again to dominate Pisan politics, it was this action that led them to accuse Ugolino of treachery and to imprison him along with his children.

**22–4** The prison in which Ugolino was confined was the *Muda* (or 'Mew') where, it is thought, the hunting birds and civic eagles of Pisa were kept during the moulting season.

**28–36** Ruggieri is the 'Master' of the hunt. The Gualandi, Sismondi and Lanfranchi were powerful families belonging to the Ghibelline faction in Pisa.

**79–90** Thebes, the city of Oedipus and subject of Statius's epic *Thebaid*, is regularly regarded by Dante as the archetypal city of corruption. (See *Inferno* 32 and *Purgatorio* 22.) Pisa was also thought to have been founded by Theban travellers. Capraia and

Gorgogna are islands off the coast of Pisa at the mouth of the Arno. If they were to drift together, Pisa would be flooded with river water.

**118–20** Frate Alberigo was a leading member of the Guelf families of Faenza and also a member of the lay order of *frati godenti* (see note to *Inferno* 23: 103–8). In 1285, he invited several members of his family with whom he was in dispute over land rights to dinner – and had them murdered. The sign he gave for the assassination was, 'Let the fruits be brought in.' Hence his reference to figs and dates. Figs are a poor fruit, dates are exotic and expensive: for his act of treachery Alberigo now receives more than abundant recompense in Hell.

**124–6** The name for the second lowest circle of treachery derives from that of Ptolemaeus, who, in 1 Maccabees 16: 11–16, is said to have assassinated Simon Maccabaeus and both of his sons at a banquet. Atropos is one of the three Fates: Clotho spins the thread of life; Lachesis measures it; Atropos severs it.

**133–8** Branca d'Oria, member of a noble Genovese family, invited his father-in-law Michel Zanche to dinner (see note to *Inferno* 22: 79–90) and had him murdered. Branca (a personal name, but also the Italian word for 'hook' and 'branch') was still alive in 1325, some four years after Dante's death.

# CANTO 34

*Giudecca, where treachery against sovereigns and benefactors is punished. Satan. The climb out of Hell through the centre of the earth.*

**1–3** These lines offer a burlesque version of the hymn '*Vexilla regis*', by Venantius Fortunatus (AD 535–600), sung in Holy Week before Easter: 'The battle standards of the King advance, / the mystery of the Cross shines out, / by which the very creator of flesh / was hung in flesh upon the gallows.' Line 1 of this canto may be translated as 'The battle standards of Hell advance'.

**28f** Satan is seen. He has betrayed the just purposes of God. But above all, like Judas, he has betrayed the creative love that is enacted in the divine relationship of the Trinity. Thus Dante's Satan is a parasitical figure, existing only as a negative image of the ultimate truth. His three faces are parodic reflections of the

Trinity. His movements are wholly different from the harmoni-
ous and productive movements of the universe that finally gather
Dante up in the concluding moments of the *Paradiso*. Evil, for
Dante, is pure negation. In the course of the *Commedia*, Dante
does not say much about Satan. But when he does, for instance
in a final brief reference in *Paradiso* 19, he stresses not rebellion
but stupidity, impatience and passivity. Satan was once Lucifer
(*Inferno* 34: 89), the highest being in Creation, who would
progressively have been given as much light as any finite creature
could possibly receive. Instead of 'waiting' for light he falls
'*acerbo*' ('unripe' (*Paradiso* 19: 46–8)). It is for this reason that,
in this canto, Satan is represented in a peculiarly mechanical and
negative form.

64–7  It is said of Judas Iscariot, the Apostle who betrayed Christ, that
'Satan entered into him' (John 13: 27). Marcus Junius Brutus
(85–42 BC) and Gaius Cassius Longinus (d. 42 BC) led the
conspiracy to assassinate Julius Caesar in 44 BC, when Caesar
sought to become emperor. Dante's view of this conspiracy is
significantly different from Shakespeare's, and it is consistent
with his increasingly imperial sympathies that he should con-
demn it as treachery. However, it is remarkable that in the next
canto of the *Commedia*, *Purgatorio* 1, a fellow opponent of
Caesar, Cato, who like Brutus and Cassius committed suicide in
defeat, should appear as the first soul in Purgatory and the
'guardian' of the purgatorial mountain. In the *Purgatorio* Dante's
standards of judgement are by no means identical to those in the
*Inferno*.

103–33  Space and time in this canto are measured from Jerusalem,
which in medieval cartography was thought of as the central
point of the northern hemisphere. It was at Jerusalem, through
Christ's crucifixion in the city (lines 112–15), that humanity was
redeemed from sin. In the southern hemisphere, at the antipodes
of Jerusalem, there is, on Dante's view, the mountain of Purga-
tory, where human beings as described in the second *cantica* of
the *Commedia* purify themselves from their earthly sins. The
formation of Purgatory is discussed at lines 121–6. On this
understanding, when it is midnight in Jerusalem, it is night in the
northern hemisphere from the Ganges to Gibraltar. Dante's jour-
ney down through Hell, which lies directly beneath Jerusalem,
began on the evening of Good Friday. It is now at the end of its
first full day, about 6 p.m. on the evening of Holy Saturday in
Jerusalem (line 68). The journey up through the empty subterra-

nean sphere, described in the second half of this canto, continues until just before dawn on Easter Sunday. The 'highest point' (line 114) is the zenith or place in the sky directly above any terrestrial point, in this case Jerusalem.